Understanding
Boat
Electronics

Understanding Boat Electronics

John C. Payne

SHERIDAN HOUSE

This edition first published 2006 by
Sheridan House Inc.
145 Palisade Street
Dobbs Ferry, NY 10522
www.sheridanhouse.com

Library of Congress Cataloging in Publication Data
Payne, John C.
    Understanding boat electronics / John C. Payne.
      p. cm.
   Includes index.
   ISBN 1-57409-228-6 (pbk. : alk. paper)
    1. Ships—Automation. 2. Electronics in navigation. I. Title.

   VM480.P39 2006
   623.8'504—dc22   2006002188

ISBN 1-57409-228-6

Printed in the United States of America

CONTENTS

1. POSITION-FIXING SYSTEMS

What is a position-fixing system?

A position-fixing system shows you where you are. No one can doubt that the advances in electronic position-fixing systems in recent years have been nothing short of spectacular. Equally the fall in GPS prices has ensured that nearly everyone can have one on board.

What is repeatable accuracy?

This is defined simply as the ability to sail back to a position or waypoint previously fixed by the receiver, and is vitally important with Man Overboard (MOB) functions. If any system is placed in a static situation, and the positions plotted at intervals, there will be a wandering of position. It is important to remember that all displayed positions must be used with the understanding that errors exist. Hitting the rocks and claiming the position-fixing system was at fault is not a valid defense.

What is predictable accuracy?

This is less concise than repeatable accuracy. Essentially this is the difference between the position indicated on your position-fixing system and that indicated on your chart. These errors are often due to the vagaries of electronic fixing systems such as signal propagation problems. They can be attributed to datum variations, inaccuracies in the electronically derived position, etc.

What happened to those earlier systems?

Many boaters are curious about the status of the various systems that used to be around. Satnav or the Transit Satellite Navigation System was switched off and its receivers cannot be converted for use with GPS. Decca has also been shut down and its receivers cannot be converted for use with GPS. Radio Direction Finding (RDF) is still in limited use; there has been considerable reorganization and reduction in stations and beacon frequencies, with fewer stations and frequencies now available. LORAN is still operational although there has been pressure to shut down the Loran system (and some chains have been shut down), but some expansion has also occurred.

All about the Global Positioning System (GPS)

The US Dept of Defense (DOD) operates the NAVSTAR system. The system consists of 24 satellites in six polar orbits so that at least four will always be visible above the horizon at any time. Twenty-one will be in operation with three used as spares.

GPS Satellite Matrix

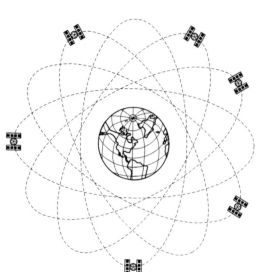

What happens when a GPS is switched on?

Turning the power on initializes with the closest satellite and ephemeris data being downloaded into memory. A period of up to 20 minutes is often required at first to stabilize a position and verify the status of satellites, availability etc. After switching off a GPS, the last position is retained in memory. If your position remains within 50 nm, prior to the next power up, a position will generally be available within about 3–5 minutes.

1. **Acquisition.** The receiver monitors data from other satellites in view. Based on data, it locks on to a satellite to commence the ranging process.

2. **Position fix.** Based on the data on positions and times the receiver calculates the position based on trilateration with respect to the positions of satellites. Normally this will be displayed to two decimal places. Some units give three decimal places, but such accuracy is highly suspect and should be treated with caution.

What is differential GPS (DGPS)?

This system is designed to overcome the position errors with respect to selective availability. It reduces errors in fixes substantially. DGPS uses a shore-based reference station located in an accurately surveyed location. The position is compared with the GPS derived position to produce an error or position offset. These errors may be due to SA or other causes. A correction signal to satellite range data (pseudo-range differential) is then broadcast by radio beacon to a radio beacon receiver. This is incorporated into the vessel GPS receiver position computation to obtain a final and more accurate position. The accuracy has come down to around 2 meters.

Wide Area Augmentation System (WAAS)

DGPS is already being "phased out" in the USA with the introduction of WAAS. The system operates by a ground base calculated ionosphere differential correction signal being uploaded to a satellite and rebroadcast back again to WAAS enabled GPS receivers. Systems are known as Satellite Differential GPS (SDGPS). Europe is developing a similar system called European Geostationary Navigation Overlay Service (EGNOS), and in Asia a system called MSAS is under development.

How accurate is GPS?

GPS accuracy has two levels.

1. **Precise Positioning Service (PPS).** This service is primarily for military use and is derived from the Precise (P) code. The P code is transmitted on the L1 (1575.42MHz) and L2 (1227.60MHz) frequencies. PPS fixes are generally accurate within 16 meters spherical error.

2. **Standard Positioning Service (SPS).** This service is for civilian use and is derived from the Course and Acquisition (C/A) code. Accuracy levels have been degraded to within 141 meters 95% of the time.

What is selective availability (SA)?

This is the deliberate process of degrading positional accuracy by altering or introducing errors in the clock data and satellite ephemeris data. SA is characterized by a wandering position, and often a course and speed over the ground of up to 1.5 knots while actually stationary. SA has been officially switched off, but it can be activated in times of defense emergencies.

What is Horizontal Dilution of Position (HDOP)?

Accuracy quality is quantified by what is called (Geometric) Horizontal Dilution of Precision (HDOP), which indicates the dilution of precision in a horizontal direction. The cause is poor satellite geometry, which is due to poor satellite distribution. It is generally measured on a scale of one to 10. The higher the number, the poorer the position confidence level.

GPS HDOP

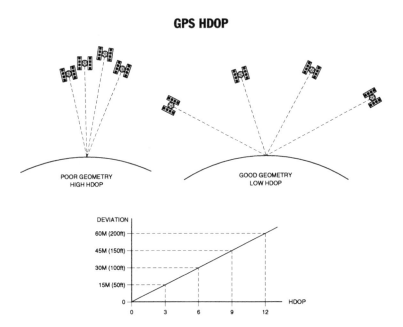

About GPS and chart datum variations

Plotting a position on a chart has inherent errors. These errors can be caused by the GPS fix error or the transformation between GPS datum and chart datum. There may be a discrepancy that requires correction, and many charts carry appropriate notes. A wide variety of chart datum are in use worldwide. New charts are generally being compiled on WGS84 datum, the same datum used by GPS. Recently an official warning was issued not to rely on any position within 3 nm of land in the Caribbean. Note that Datum NAS83 on US charts is the same as WGS84 (GPS) datum on UK charts.

What causes GPS errors?

GPS is considered by many boaters to be an accurate navigation source but it does have inherent errors that decrease accuracy. These errors are in addition to the HDOP and SA factors previously mentioned.

1. **GPS clock errors.** Each GPS satellite has two rubidium and two cesium atomic clocks. These clocks are monitored against terrestrial atomic clocks. Based on this information, the entire GPS system is continually calibrated against UTC.

2. **Ionosphere effects.** Like radio signals, both ionosphere and troposphere conditions can affect GPS accuracy. Errors occur in signal transmission times that can impose signal propagation delays. This signal refraction introduces timing errors that cause positional inaccuracies. Like radio propagation it alters with changes in atmospheric conditions, solar activity, etc. Errors can be as great as 20-30 meters during the day and 5 meters at night.

3. **Multipath effects.** This occurs when signals from a satellite traveling to a receiver arrive at slightly different times due to reflection or alteration. The effect is that positions may be derived off the "bad" signal, resulting in inaccuracy.

4. **Satellite integrity.** If the signal being transmitted from a satellite is corrupt due to a malfunction, it will have subsequent effects on position computations and solutions.

What is the GLONASS Positioning System?

The Russian system nominally operates with a 24-satellite system, however this is down to 7–8 only. The claims are that the system is more accurate than GPS, and this has been proven in higher latitude locations such as the UK and Europe. There are now dual GLONASS and GPS receivers and offshore oil industry positioning frequently uses both.

About GPS satellite acquisition modes

1. **Single channel, sequential.** A single-channel receiver reduces receiver costs. Position updates are made every 10–15 seconds because a single-channel receiver must search for, interrogate, and acquire satellites in sequential order. This method is slow and in bad weather can cause some problems. In rough weather, when the vessel is subject to considerable movement, the receiver has problems acquiring and locking onto satellites, with resultant position degradation. These types of receivers generally take some time to acquire their first fix, typically from 10 to 20 minutes and longer.

2. **Dual channel, sequential.** These common types of receivers use two channels to track several satellites and they process two channels sequentially. Accuracy is very good and the time-to-first-fix (TTFF) is generally very fast, typically around 5 minutes. On some two-channel units, one channel ranges, which speeds up position processing, while the other channel downloads ephemeris.

3. **Multiple channel, parallel processing.** Multiple-channel units are now virtually standard. This powerful processing capability enables the monitoring and tracking of up to 12 satellites and the parallel processing of all those satellites in view simultaneously. These units increase position accuracy, reduce errors, and improve the HDOP. The TTFF in these units is very fast; in fact, TTFF can be achieved in several seconds. Many handheld receivers now incorporate parallel processing, and it is by far the better system to choose. In rough weather conditions, fix integrity and accuracy will generally be very high.

4. **Multiplex processing.** Multiplex systems use one or two channels to sequentially handle satellites at high processing speeds. They are sometimes referred to as pseudo-multi-channel systems because performance under ideal conditions is nearly as fast and accurate as that of true multiple-channel systems. The high speed sampling and processing of ephemeris occurs concurrently with the ranging function.

How does space weather affect GPS?

The ionosphere is well known for the effects it has on HF and ham radio. A lot less known are the effects on GPS. It is an important source of range and range rate errors for users of GPS satellites where high accuracy is required. Ionosphere range error can vary from a few meters to tens of meters, with troposphere range error at a peak up to 2–3 meters. The ionosphere has a dispersive effect. It can alter rapidly in value, changing significantly over one day. In practice the troposphere range error does not alter more the + or – 10% over long periods. GPS signals pass through the ionosphere but suffer propagation delays. Ranging errors of tens of meters can occur in extreme ionosphere conditions; typically it is 5–10 meters. These generally equatorial events are often associated with plasma bubbles that characterize the unstable state of the equatorial ionosphere at night.

What are plasma bubbles?

Ionosphere plasma bubbles are a natural phenomenon consisting of wide regions within the atmosphere where there are large depletions of the ionosphere plasma. They were first detected in Brazil in 1976 and continue to be a major problem within their offshore oil industry, and are subject to much research. Plasma bubbles are known to interfere with satellite communications in the frequency range VHF to 6GHz, and are known to interfere with GPS causing position errors. The plasma bubbles are closely aligned with the earth's geomagnetic field lines along which they may extend for thousands of kilometers and across geomagnetic field lines, they measure 100–400 kms. They occur after sunset and exist at nights only. There is generally more activity during periods of maximum solar activity.

What is scintillation?

Irregularities in the ionosphere produce diffraction and refraction effects, causing short-term signal fading. This can severely stress the tracking capabilities of the GPS receiver. Signal enhancements also occur, but the GPS user cannot get any benefit from brief periods of strong signal. Fading can be so severe that the signal level will drop completely below the receiver lock threshold and must be continually re-acquired. The effects are called ionospheric scintillations, and the region can cover up to 50% of the earth in varying degrees. Strong scintillation effects in near equatorial regions are observed generally one hour after sunset to midnight. Precise measurement using GPS should if possible be avoided from 7 to 12 PM local time during periods of high solar activity and during months of normal high scintillation activity. There are also seasonal and solar cycle effects that reduce chances of encountering scintillation in near equatorial regions. From April to August, the chances are small of significant scintillation in the American, African and Indian regions. In the Pacific region, scintillation effects maximize during these months. From September to March the situation reverses. The regions where the strongest scintillation effects are observed are Kwajalein Island in the Pacific and Ascension Island in the South Atlantic. The occurrence of strong amplitude scintillation is also closely correlated with the sunspot number; in years with near minimum solar activity, there are little if any strong scintillation effects on GPS. Where GPS is used for autopilot waypoint steering in these regions, skippers should be alert for course changes, and for unexplainable and short-term periods of inaccuracy.

How to troubleshoot your GPS

The reliability and accuracy of your GPS system depends on a proper installation. Now that most boats have GPS as their primary navigation source, it is essential they be properly installed.

1. **Check the aerial installation.** Aerials should be sited so that they are clear of fly bridge frames, spars, deck equipment and other radio aerials. Where possible, the aerial should have as wide a field of view as practicable, while being located as low as possible. In installations that utilize a mast or stern post with mounted radar, ensure that the GPS aerial is not within the beam spread of the radar antenna. Make sure that the location is not prone to fouling by ropes and other equipment that may damage the aerial.

2. **Check the cabling.** Many GPS problems are a result of cabling problems. Power supply cables should be routed as far as practicable from equipment cables carrying high currents. Aerial cables should also be routed well clear. It is extremely important for the aerial cable not to be kinked, bent, or placed in any tight radius. This has the effect of narrowing the dielectric gap within the coaxial cable, which may cause signal problems. Make sure that all through-deck glands are high quality to properly protect the cable and keep water from going below. Thrudex (Index) makes cable glands that enable the plug to be passed through along with the cable. Do not shorten or lengthen an aerial cable unless your manufacturer approves it.

3. **Check the connectors.** Make sure all connectors are properly inserted into the GPS receiver. Ensure that screw-retaining rings are tight, because plugs can work loose and cause intermittent contact. The coaxial connector from the aerial into the receiver should be rotated properly so that it is locked in. External aerial connections should be made water resistant where possible. Use of self-amalgamating tape is a useful method for doing this. If you have to remove and refit an aerial connector, ensure that you use considerable care and assemble the connector in accordance with the manufacturer's instructions. Use a multimeter on the resistance range, and check the center pin to shield resistance. Low resistance generally means a shorted shield strand. Resistance is typically 50–150 ohms.

   Grounding. The ground connection provided with the system must be connected to the RF ground system or negative supply polarity depending on manufacturer's recommendations.

4. **Check the power supply.** A clean power supply is essential to proper operation. Use either an in-line filter or install suppressors across "noisy" motors and alternator. The power supply should not come from a battery used for engine starting, or used with any high current equipment such as an anchor windlass or electric toilet. Note that many cheaper unsuppressed fluorescent lights also cause interference that may create data corruption.

What GPS maintenance is required?

Perform the following routine maintenance checks. Many problems can be identified and rectified before the system fails.

1. Check the aerial to make sure the connections are tight and the plugs in good condition. Ensure that it is mounted vertically and has not been pushed over, a common problem.

2. Ensure that all connectors are properly inserted. In particular, examine the external aerial connector for signs of corrosion, especially the outer shield braiding.

3. Many GPS units have internal lithium batteries with a life span of only around 3 years so make sure that the battery is renewed on time.

4. Make a hard copy list of all waypoints for reference and reprogramming if required.

How to do basic GPS troubleshooting

Many problems are related to peripheral equipment rather than the unit, and simple checks may save considerable sums of money.

1. **Large fix error.** The GPS system may be down, or a satellite may be shut down. Check your NAVTEX transmissions or other navigation information source for news of outages. SA may be activated, or the HDOP may simply be excessive due to poor satellite geometry in your location. With sequential receivers, loss of signal may be a problem in heavy sea states.

2. **Small fix error.** Errors that are not significantly large are attributable to a number of sources. The signal may be subject to an excessive amount of atmospheric disturbances, such as periods of extensive solar flare activity. This may be confirmed by similar HF reception difficulties, which also suffer propagation problems. The aerial connections and part of the installation may have degraded, so check the entire system. Make sure aerial orientation is vertical and not partially pushed over. Check that some aerial shadowing has not been introduced.

3. **No fix.** This is often caused in sequential receivers by loss of a satellite view or when a satellite goes out of service. Another common cause is the aerial being pushed over to horizontal, so check that it is vertical. Aerial damage from having been struck by equipment is another major cause of a sudden fix loss. Check all cables and connections. If these show no defects, a check of all initialization parameters may be necessary; if those check out, the receiver and aerial may need servicing.

4. **Data corruption.** This is often due to power supply problems. Check whether the incident coincides with engine or machinery run periods. Radiated interference is also a possibility, often from radio equipment. A lightning strike with resultant electromagnetic pulse can also cause similar problems. Another quite common cause of data corruption is that caused by "fingers." Has another person unfamiliar with operating the GPS altered configuration parameters such as time settings or altitude?

GPS troubleshooting

Large fix error: GPS satellite system down; Selective availability switched on; High HDOP; Severe atmospheric problem; Satellite acquisition loss (heavy weather)

Small fix error: Atmospheric propagation problem; Aerial shadowing

No fix: GPS satellite system down; Aerial fault; Aerial cable fault; Aerial pushed over to horizontal; Aerial "view" obstructed'

Data corruption: Power supply interference; Radiated interference

About LORAN-C

Loran-C is a long range pulsed low-frequency hyperbolic land-based radio aid. The system relies on the accurate measurement of the time difference of radio signals received from a master and slave transmitters to derive a hyperbolic position line. With two position lines or more, a position fix can be made based on the intersection on lines of position.

About differential LORAN–C (dLORAN)

This system has escaped shutdown due to the effects of 9/11 and the need for a redundant navigation system. This is a handheld unit and the differential signal is within an additional 9th pulse in the LORAN-C signal.

About LORAN errors

Loran-C is prone to a range of errors.

1. **Skywave and groundwave effect.** Loran signals travel via a ground wave, which is the shortest path. Other paths also occur, that include several skywave types. Depending on time of day, skywaves may be even stronger than ground-waves, but they always arrive after groundwaves. At chain extremities the stronger skywaves may be stronger than weak groundwaves giving errors up to 10 nm.

2. **Lightning impulses.** Pulses from lightning can distort or corrupt signals.

About LORAN installation

Correct installation is the key to optimum performance.

1. **Antenna and coupler location.** Correct installation away from electrical equipment and other antennas is necessary. Clearance is ideally a minimum of 6 feet. On motor boats either a separate whip antenna or alternatively an insulated backstay can be used.

2. **Grounding.** The grounding factor is as important as the antenna. This can be the RF ground plate used by other electronics equipment. The grounding wire should be at least 12 AWG.

3. **Interference.** Interference is the major cause of fix errors. Loran C is sensitive to noise in the 90–110kHz spectrum. Common causes are fluorescent lights, alternators, tachometers, and radars. Suppression methods are outlined in that chapter, and all should be installed. Generally you can test for noise problems using receiver diagnostics to check Signal to Noise Ratio (SNR). With alternators recommended capacitor is a 10,000-microfarad electrolytic rated at 50V.

About Radio Direction Finding

RDF has rapidly lost its place with the emergence of GPS. There has been a dramatic reduction in beacons and also beacon frequency rationalization. The call sign of the station must be identified correctly before taking a bearing. Most VHF RDF stations in the UK and Europe are for emergency use only during SAR operations.

2 ELECTRONIC CHARTING

All about electronic charting

Most chart plotters universally now incorporate GPS, or conversely are included within GPS units, and are effectively position-fixing devices for many. The chart plotter is essentially a display with processor that decodes the data on the chart cartridges for display on the screen. The information is often layered so that chart areas can be expanded. The lights, buoyage and contours can be called up as required. There are many functions and stored data available. They can include tidal predictions; sun and moon rise and set, Navaids such as lights and buoys (10,000 plus items is typical), waypoints and routes (1000/20 is typical). DSC radio interfacing is also possible showing the location of a vessel in distress. One important feature is sets that use standard chart cartography as some use proprietary software that may not be easily obtainable. There are many features to consider that include drag and drop waypoints, active route waypoint insertion and deletion, and the ability to store routes, and fast redraw times, typically 0.5 to 3 seconds. Cartography features should include clear chart scale indication, clear direction indication when not in North-up mode, an indication when over-zoomed, good buoy visibility and identification, clearly visible and identifiable land features and contours, the use of standard labelling conventions on features, the display of drying heights, the ability to edit contours and shaded depth contours. One important factor is the ability to update and also some identification when the chart was last updated, similar to paper charts. It is important that any unit be user friendly, and has intuitive controls, menus, soft keys and dedicated keys.

Chart plotter displays

Systems now use high-resolution monochrome (gray) LCD displays, or full color active matrix TFT (Thin Film Transistor) displays. Screen display quality or resolution is determined by pixels, i.e. 480 x 350. The greater the number of pixels, the greater the resolution, and the price also increases. Power consumption is typically 6W (0.5 amps). To get the most from dedicated plotters or computer-based software plotting, make sure you read and understand the manual and practice. Trying to learn while under way is both dangerous and distracting. There is a trend in larger motorboats and sailing yachts to have PC based systems with remote sunlight viewable displays, for pilothouse and fly bridge. Many displays are flat-screen LCD types with SVGA resolution, and external standard ones are waterproof to NEMA 4 standard and are rated up to a brightness of more than 1,600 nit which is some 1000% brighter than a laptop.

About cartography systems

The cartographic chart data systems are based on memory chips or more correctly EPROM (Electronically Programmable Read Only Memory) or CD-Rom. There are many formats that include M-93, S-57, NDI and Navionics. Several manufacturers use a specific format or protocol.

1. **Raster Charts.** A raster chart is identical to the paper chart, and originates from original government master charts. ARCS (Admiralty Raster Chart Service) charts are supplied on a CD-Rom. Maptech uses raster scan charts and works with the NOAA to produce official charts. Seafarer are identical to ARCS and are produced by the Australian Hydrographic Office for Australian waters.

2. **Vector Charts.** The scanning of paper charts to create a raster image produces a vector chart. These are then vectorized to store data in layers, which allows easy zooming in on detail. They do not resemble conventional charts. The advantages over raster charts are much faster screen update rates.

   a. **C-Map NT+.** These vector-based charts are stored on solid-state memory cards that include C-Cards and PCMCIA cards.

   b. **Garmin Blue Chart Cartography.** These are based on Transas data. G-Map is for the new plotters and is available on CD-ROM also.

   c. **Navionics.** These are known as Gold XL3 charts. They come in MMC or compact flash cards and suit Humminbird, Lowrance and Raymarine plotters. Charts are typically 128Mb and smaller regions use 32Mb.

About chart corrections and updates

Chart corrections and updates are now part of standard services and are offered by Maptech for NOAA charts. They require up-to-date Notices to Mariners, although you can do that via Internet for free. Cartridges can be updated every couple of years.

About PC charting software

Software developments for electronic charting have been rapid with packages offering very powerful navigation tools. There are varying features and capabilities; purchasing decisions will depend on them. Software features include the ability to display multiple chart windows; the ability to rotate charts; passage planning showing hazards; the display of tidal heights and streams and planning; the ability to interface using NMEA to autopilot, radar, GPS and instruments; the ability to overlay radar and display ARPA targets.

1. **Nobeltech.** The most popular products are the Visual Navigation Suite (VNS) and the Nobeltech Admiral. They are compatible for use with Passport Deluxe, BSB formatted charts, and SoftChart. They offer many features including unlimited tracking capabilities, tide and current overlays. VNS also offers ARPA/MARPA and AIS target tracking capabilities.

2. **RayMarine RNS 5.0.** This package offers simultaneous raster and vector viewing capability. It also permits animated weather satellite images overlaid on chart, and communications with SeaTalk systems allowing full chart plotter functionality.

3. ECHOSOUNDERS, FISHFINDERS AND SONAR

What is an echosounder?

The echo- or depth-sounder is an important and indispensable piece of electronics. I have spent considerable time working with underwater acoustics systems in the offshore oil industry, and a couple of years working on a submarine sonar program, and I can say that this technology is very complex. Equipment performance depends on the output power of the transmitter, the efficiency of the transducer, the sensitivity of the receiver along with the processing software that filters out the spurious noise. Many fishfinders have user selectable noise filters to enhance noise rejection processing. The price of equipment reflects all of these elements, with the most expensive systems having the highest performance specifications on all factors.

What is SONAR?

The word SONAR is derived from SOund, NAvigation and Ranging and has its origins in the Second World War in anti-submarine warfare. The depth sounder normally projects the acoustic signal directly downwards at a set beam angle so that a cone of coverage is made with respect to the bottom or contours being passed over. Most depth sounders operate at a frequency of 200kHz, lower transmission frequencies give greater depth capability, although the EchoPilot operates at 150kHz and B & G at 183kHz.

    1. **Digital.** The most common depth instrument is a vertical unit with a digital or analog display incorporating depth alarms, anchor watch alarm facilities, etc. The information displayed is generally several seconds old due to signal processing times.

2. **Keel Offset.** This adjustment is important so that the depth of the water under the keel is measured; it is surprising how many installations have this inaccurately set. Read the manual and adjust the offset accurately.

How accurate is a depth sounder?

Acoustic signals suffer from propagation delays and attenuation as water and various bottom formations cause absorption, scattering, refraction and reflection. Biological matter such as algae and plankton as well as suspended particulate matter such as silt, dissolved minerals and salts can cause this. The water density and salinity levels as well as water temperatures all affect signal propagation. Cold layers of water called thermoclines can affect signal; this is more relevant to deep water. Bottom formations consisting of sand and mud, or large quantities of weed beds will absorb or scatter signal. Hard bottoms that comprise shale, sand and rock will reflect signal with strong returns. The power output of a unit is also important with respect to range and resolution, the higher the power the greater the depth range and signal return.

Depth Transducer

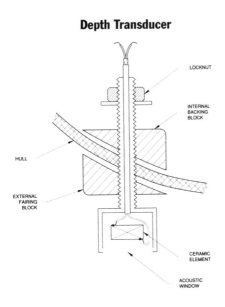

What is a fishfinder?

The basic principle is that an electrical signal is converted to an acoustic signal via a piezoelectric element (crystal) and is transmitted towards the sea bottom. Transducers are typically constructed of a crystal composed of various elements that include lead, zirconate, barium, titanate and conductive coatings. Some fishfinders have transmission power ratings up to 1000W. When the transducer transmits the acoustic signal it expands to form a cone-shaped characteristic. When the acoustic signal strikes a fish or seabed it is reflected back. The shape and diameter of a transducer determines the cone angle. The acoustic signal strength is at maximum along the center axis of the cone, and decreases away from it. The cone angle is based on the power at the center to a point where the power decreases to -3db, with the total angle being measured from -3db point on each side. Most manufacturers offer models with a variety of cone angles; wide cone angles have less depth capability with wider coverage, while small cone angles give greater depth penetration with reduced area coverage. High Frequency transducers (190 kHz) are available in either wide or narrow cone angles. Low frequency transducers have cone angles in the range 30–45 degrees. The further away from the centerline of the cone, the less strong return echoes are. This can be improved by increasing the sensitivity control. While most fishfinders have a single beam, manufacturers such as Humminbird are now introducing multi-beam systems that have several sonar beams ranging from 2 to 6. This subsequently increases the coverage area, and accuracy. The Single Beam system has a cone angle of 16–24 degrees, which gives a depth of 600–1000 feet. The Dual Beam system has ranges up to 2000 feet. The first beam is in the cone center, and a second beam surrounds it to increase the coverage area. The Tri-Beam systems have a 90-degree coverage area with ranges up to 1000 feet. The main beam is directed down, and two beams are configured to each side to give a large coverage area. The Wide Side has 3 beams to view bank and bottom contours with the center beam directed down 120 feet and port and starboard to 120 feet. The Six Beam system gives a 3D contour display of the sea bottom; Lowrance systems give a coverage of 53 degrees up to a depth of 240 feet.

Transducer Beam Angles

Single Beam

Dual Beam

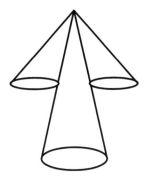

Tri-Beam

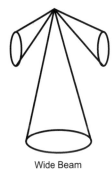

Wide Beam

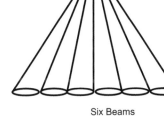

Six Beams

What is transducer cavitation?

Cavitation is caused by water turbulence passing over a transducer head, and affects transducer performance. At slow speeds the laminar flow is smooth without any interference; however at speed air bubbles are created over the transducer face affecting acoustic signal transmission and reception. The effect is to interfere with transmitted acoustic signals that reflect back off the bubbles, which effectively causes noise and masks signals. Turbulence is caused by hull form or obstructions, water flow over the transducer, and propulsion. Transom mounted units must be carefully mounted to avoid turbulence from outboard motors or water flow off the transom. The higher the speed the greater the turbulence; riveted alloy boats have turbulence off each rivet head. Manufacturers are designing transducers that work better at higher speeds, including transducers with improved hydrodynamic shapes. Transducers must be mounted in areas of little turbulence or clear of hull flow areas, which is not always easy.

About frequencies and power output

Transmission frequency affects both the depth range and cone angle. The speed of sound in water is a constant of 4800 ft per second, and the time between the transmission and reception of the returned signal is measured to give a range or depth figure. Lowrance has a frequency of 192kHz and a deepwater one of 50kHz. Simrad units have a user selectable tri-frequency capability of 38/50, 38/200 or 50/200kHz with depth range up to 1800 meters, and a maximum ping rate of 15 per second. Shallow waters less than 300 feet give the best results with high frequency transducers of 200kHz and wide cone angles up to 20 degrees. In depths greater than 300 feet low frequency transducers of 50kHz with small cone angles of 8 degrees are the best option. Furuno has introduced the Free Synthesizer (FFS) Transceiver on the FCV 1200 Color Video Sounder, with frequency and output power user selectable. The dual-frequency sounder has output settings of 15, 28, 38, 50, 88, 107 and 200kHz. Power outputs are quoted in watts, some quote peak-to-peak. The use of watts RMS is more accurate, typically within the range 100–600 watts.

About fishfinder displays

The most common display type is the Liquid Crystal Display (LCD), Lowrance has what is called Film SuperTwist and Humminbird use FSTN displays that use black and not blue or tan pixels. Displays must be both high resolution and good contrast and are typically in the range of 240 and 320 vertical pixels. Displays are also sometimes quoted in pixels per square inch, i.e. 15,170, and the more pixels the better the resolution. The LCD display comprises a complex grid of pixels, small square display elements that include a screen image. Pixels are turned on or off to form an image on the screen, and return echoes are processed and displayed as dark pixels. Grayscale display images in several shades of gray to indicate signal strength variations, with strong signals being very dark and weak ones light gray. Each successive return activates a new column of pixels so that a continuous image is displayed on the screen as each column is replaced. The display resolution quality is dependent on the number of pixels in each vertical column. The number of horizontal pixels determines the retention period that a displayed image is on the screen. This also determines the ability of a system to support additional image windows in a split screen mode. Some units have high-resolution displays in 8 or 16 colors on a 10.4-inch TFT LCD display. Color displays use up to 16 colors for different signal strengths, the stronger ones are displayed in red, and weaker signals as green or blue, for example baitfish schools are generally in blue or green, with larger game fish being yellow, orange or red. The seabed and wrecks are usually displayed as dark orange or red.

What is the whiteline function?

All fishfinders have a feature called grayline or whiteline that assists in discriminating bottom hardness from the bottom contours. The bottom is displayed as a thin dark line with a gray area below it. Thin lines and thick gray areas represent hard bottoms, and a thick black line with no gray represents soft bottoms. This allows targeting of precise bottom formations for specific fish types. The grayline feature on Lowrance fishfinders allows differentiation between soft and hard bottom types. The feature "paints" gray on bottom targets that have a stronger signal return than preset values. A soft mud type bottom will have a relatively weak return and this is displayed as a narrow gray line. Hard rock bottoms will have a strong return and be represented with a wide gray line.

What does the zoom function do?

The zoom function allows the magnification of a portion of the depth range to improve analysis and identification of targets in that area. The typical magnification scales are x2 and x4 the normal scale. This allows monitoring of a certain depth range such as 40 to 50 feet, or zooming on the bottom and 10 feet above it. The split screen feature allows tracking of different features simultaneously such as zoom segment and the bottom contour.

What does the sensitivity control do?

The sensitivity control enables the receiver to tune in or tune out returns. If the unit is set with low sensitivity, it will not detect bottom details, fish or obstruction. If it is set with high sensitivity, it will return signals on everything and will clutter the screen with spurious returns. Sensitivity should be adjusted so that bottom is clearly defined along with white or gray line and some surface clutter. Most fishfinders have automatic sensitivity adjustment, which compensates for ambient water conditions and depth. Lowrance has Advanced Signal Processing (ASP) which uses complex software to process parameters such as water conditions, noise and interference levels, boat speed to automatically adjust control settings to optimize the images on the display. This entails setting the sensitivity to the highest level possible without allowing noise to be displayed, creating a balance between noise rejection and sensitivity. Submarine sonar systems use extremely sophisticated signal processors and software and this approach is very similar. The sea is a very dynamic environment and sound travels very great distances. The acoustics signals can be absorbed and reflected. The higher the frequencies the greater scattering effects, and the lower the frequency the greater the range. Wave actions, microorganisms, varying salt densities and suspended solids further enhance signal scattering.

About water temperature and thermoclines

Water temperature affects fish, as they are cold-blooded animals, and they have the same temperature as the surrounding water. Due to biological factors, fish feeding and spawning behavior is dependent on water temperature, so that fish are generally found at locations where the water temperature suits activities. Any body of water consist of layers, the surface is generally warmer than the middle or bottom layers. The interface between areas of different temperature is called a thermocline. Thermoclines are important for locating fish as they tend to be found either just above or below them. Fishfinders can detect thermoclines; the greater the difference in temperatures the more visible it becomes.

What are fish arches?

The display of fish arches on the screen is directly related to sonar acoustic characteristics. As a fish enters the acoustic cone a display pixel is turned on, and as it moves towards the center of the cone the distance between the transducer and fish decreases so that pixels are progressively turned on and display a shallower depth and therefore a stronger signal. When the fish reaches the cone center this forms half the arch, and the other half is completed as the fish moves towards the outer edge of the cone. Very small fish probably will not arch at all. Because of water conditions such as heavy surface clutter or thermoclines, the sensitivity sometimes cannot be turned up enough to get fish arches. For the best results, turn the sensitivity up as high as possible without getting too much noise on the screen. In medium to deep water, this method should work to display fish arches. If the fish does not pass through the cone center the arch will either be partial or not be displayed. Arches are not formed in shallower waters as the cone angle becomes too narrow. Arches are not formed when the boat is drifting or anchored. Fish schools vary in displayed shape depending on how much of the school is within the cone. In deeper water each fish if large enough may have an arch displayed. Fish arches are created when the cone of sound passes over a fish. The distance to a fish when the cone first strikes it is shown as A. When the center of the cone strikes the fish, the distance is shorter as shown in B. As the cone leaves the fish, the distance increases again as shown in C. The size of fish arches depends on the sensitivity adjustments, the boat speed, the water depth and cone angle, and location of the fish within the cone.

Fish Arches (Lowrance Fishfinder)

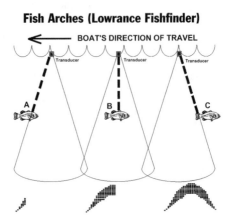

What is a forward looking sonar?

The most identifiable is the very impressive EchoPilot. These systems have benefited greatly from developments in processing power and speed. The units consist of a powerful processing unit, which enables real time processing of data. This is different from the normal depth sounder, which has an inherent delay of typically up to 16 seconds. The transducer head scans from vertical to horizontal with a beam width of 15 degrees and can "see" up to 150–200 meters forward. Maximum range depends on water depth and seabed contours, with a shoaling bottom being easier to see than one that is level or deepening. Like all sonar and depth transducers the head must be clear of turbulence. These units operate at 200kHz; two units operating close together will cause corruption of data. Also it is important to note other depth sounders and fishfinder frequencies. If all 3 are at 200kHz problems will arise; only one can be reliably operated and the others switched off.

About transducer installation

Be very careful not to bump the transducer and possibly damage the crystal element. Most installations are through hull mounted on a fairing block to ensure that the beam is facing directly down on an even keel, and to reduce any water flow turbulence. Locate in an area of minimal turbulence. Water bubbles from turbulence are a common cause of problems. In some cases they are mounted inside the hull within an oil bath or epoxy fastened to the hull on fiberglass boats. There is a sacrifice in maximum depths, which can reach 60–70% reduction in range and therefore should be avoided where possible.

About transducer stern mounting

Many powerboats also mount the transducer on a retractable bracket on the stern or transom. This arrangement while effective and less work on smaller vessels is not ideal on bigger ones. Turbulence from the propellers, and laminar flow breaking away from the hull generally affect operation and it is only effective at very low speeds.

About transducer cable installation

Always ensure that cables are installed clear of heavy current carrying cables or radio aerial cables. Never install next to log cables as is generally done, as the interference problem can be significant.

About maintenance and troubleshooting

The transducer is the only item that can be maintained, and if not, will dramatically reduce performance. Cleaning is essential, and regular removal of growth off the transducer should be undertaken. Do not bump it or apply any impact to the surface. Avoid applying antifouling to the transducer surface, as it includes small voids and air bubbles, which will reduce sensitivity. If necessary, smear on a very thin layer with your finger. Troubleshooting often entails reading the manual and determining whether settings and operating procedures are correct. Go into settings or options menu and ensure settings are on auto or defaulting to factory settings.

Check the connections

Check all connectors and connector pins for damage, and make sure that they are straight and not bent. If straightened the pins might break as they are brittle. Connectors not properly inserted or tightened up are prone to saltwater ingress and corrosion.

Check the cables

Check all cables for damage, cuts or fatigue. The transom mounted transducer cables are prone to damage and on some smaller fishing boats the transducer hull cables may be damaged.

Check the power supply

Connection problems are the major cause, either at the supply panel, or at the battery. Check the power at the plug using a multimeter set. Check should be made with engine on or off. If the engine voltmeter shows normal charge voltages, and battery checks out then it is in the intermediate connections.

What about interference?

If the fishfinder has interference, turn off all other equipment and then turn engine off. Progressively start up engine and then other equipment to determine the source, and the power supply may require suppression. Check that two fishfinders are not being run at the same time, and two vessels in very close proximity may also cause mutual interference if using similar acoustic frequencies. If the interference is present with all systems off, the fishfinder automatic noise rejection facility maybe malfunctioning.

Inspecting the transducer

Inspect the transducer for damage, marine growth, antifouling paints, and clean off the surfaces using soapy water. Do not use heavy abrasives or chisels to clean the face.

4. RADAR

What is radar?

RADAR is an acronym for RAdio Detection And Ranging. Radar can be defined as a method of locating the presence of a target, and calculating the range and angular position with respect to the radar transmitter. For closing landfalls, navigating channels and poor visibility, radar units make navigation a lot easier. Radar is not redundant with the GPS. Radar indicates where things are, while GPS indicates where you are. As a navigational aid, radar offers many very useful functions:

1. Position-fixing from geographical points.

2. Positions of other vessels.

3. Positions of buoys.

4. Land formations when trying to make a landfall in poor visibility.

5. Rain and squall locations.

6. Collision avoidance at night and in poor visibility.

Koden 24-nm Radar Display

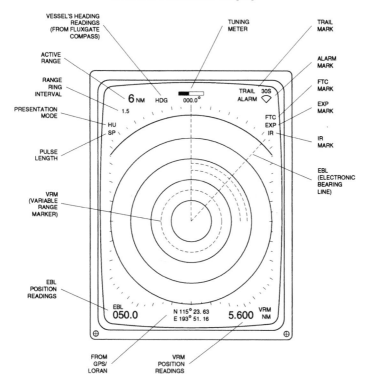

VESSEL'S HEADING READINGS (FROM FLUXGATE COMPASS)

TUNING METER

TRAIL MARK

ACTIVE RANGE

ALARM MARK

RANGE RING INTERVAL

FTC MARK

PRESENTATION MODE

EXP MARK

PULSE LENGTH

IR MARK

VRM (VARIABLE RANGE MARKER)

EBL (ELECTRONIC BEARING LINE)

EBL POSITION READINGS

6 NM   HDG   000.0°   TRAIL   30S
                        ALARM

1.5

HU
SP   FTC
                                      EXP
                                      IR

EBL   N 115° 23. 63   VRM
050.0   E 193° 51. 16   5.600   NM

FROM GPS/ LORAN

VRM POSITION READINGS

How does radar work?

Radar transmits a pulse of Radio Frequency (RF) energy. This is radiated from a highly directional rotating transmitter called the scanner. Any reflected energy is then received and processed to form an image. The time interval between transmission of the signal and reception of reflected energy can be processed to give target distance and bearing. The subject of radar reflection theory is complex. If radar is to be fully utilized it is essential to understand the behavior of radar signals on varying target materials.

Why are some scanners different?

In practice the longer the scanner the narrower the beam width, which gives better target discrimination. Of the two main scanner types, beam widths of enclosed scanners are always larger than open types. This factor is one of the trade-offs that has to be considered when selecting a radar unit. If it can be accommodated, an open scanner is far more preferable in terms of performance.

What are the scanner types?

Enclosed array type scanners are commonly installed. There are two basic types of antenna elements in use:

1. **Printed Circuit Board.** Printed circuit board phased antenna arrays are commonly fitted to enclosed scanners. The antenna is on a circuit board instead of the more expensive slotted waveguides.

2. **Slotted Waveguide.** Center fed slotted waveguide arrays are normally used on open array antennas and on larger range radomes.

About open scanners

The traditional open array scanner is more suited to motorboats and offers significant advantages. An open scanner has a beam width nearly half that of enclosed units and as such gives far better target discrimination. As mentioned earlier, the longer the scanner the better the bearing resolution. If you can tolerate an open scanner then opt for one, the improved performance is worth it. On motorboats the open scanner is far more practicable without the issues that sailing vessels have with weight and snagging of ropes.

What is side lobe attenuation?

Beam widths are not precisely cut off. There are zones outside the main beam where power is wasted and dissipated. End slotted waveguides are often used in new radars to suppress side lobes. The main problem caused by side lobes is the generating of false echoes, which are more pronounced at increased sensitivity on short ranges.

About radar frequencies

All small boat radars operate on microwave frequencies in what is termed the X band. Frequency ranges are 9200 to 9500MHz, which is a wavelength of around 3 cm. Large commercial vessels also have S-band radars.

What do the output power ratings mean?

Power ratings are given for the actual microwave output power, and a 16-mile radar is typically 1.5kW; 24 nm–2.2kW; 36 & 48nm–4kW; 64nm–6kW and 72 nm–12kW. This can be likened to a kitchen microwave, which operates on a similar principle. Given the effect microwaves have on food, the warning on eye protection should be followed. It is quite common on naval vessels with high power radars to have any bird life in the rigging incinerated when radars are started up.

About range discrimination

Range discrimination or resolution is a function of transmission pulse length. This is the minimum distance between two targets on the same bearing, which are shown as two targets. Where the distance between targets is longer than the pulse length they are shown as separate. When the distance between targets is less than the pulse length, they will appear as one target. Most radars automatically alter pulse length with a change in range settings.

What are beam angles?

Radar transmissions are similar to the light beam from a lighthouse, with a beam that has a defined angle in both vertical and horizontal planes. The beam width is normally defined as the angle over which the power is at least half of maximum output.

1. **Horizontal.** Horizontal beam widths open scanners are in the range 1.2°–2.5° and closed radomes are greater at 3.9°–7°.

2. **Vertical.** Vertical beam widths are all typically in the range 25° to 30°. The larger the width the better the performance under heeling conditions. It must be remembered that there is always a blind spot around the vessel; and very close targets may not be seen as they are inside the minimum range.

How important is the trim angle?

The trim of a motorboat or sailing yacht, and therefore the scanner, has an adverse effect on performance. As most radars have vertical beam angles of around 25°, at any heel angle there will degradation on the windward side, creating a blind spot. This is common when rolling in a beam sea where there is reflection off the backs of passing waves. Trim both fore and aft also affects performance. When a vessel is up on the plane, a radar installed level when stopped will be virtually useless, as the beam will point skywards when under way. It should be installed so that in normal conditions the beam is 12½° above and below the horizon. It should be noted that at low speeds, the beam will angle downwards significantly affecting range, and may be only useful on short range settings.

Radar Heeling Angles

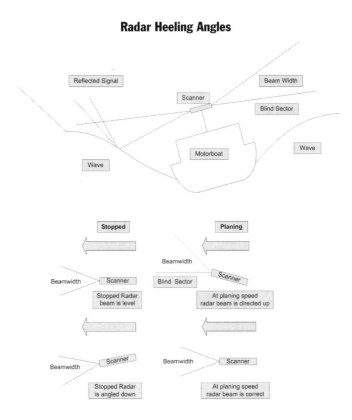

About target discrimination

Target discrimination or resolution is a function of beam width. A scanner with a narrow beam width is effectively slicing and sampling sectors of approximately 2.5° around the azimuth. Large targets will be sampled a number of times and their size quantified. A wider beam width will sample an area twice that size, and will not always discriminate between two or more targets. If a harbor entrance is narrow the radar beam may in fact see it as part of the breakwater until the range has closed up. Two targets at the same distance and close together may appear as one at longer ranges.

Target Discrimination

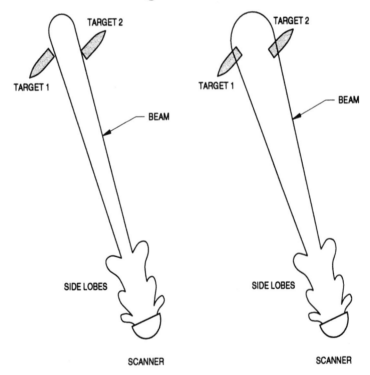

What is the radar horizon?

Maximum radar ranges are a function of both aerial and target height. Radar returns are affected by the target characteristics and also atmospheric conditions. Standard conditions are a pressure of 1013mb, temperature at sea level of 30°C, and a relative humidity of 60%. The formula for 3 cm radars for calculating radar horizon distance is RH in nm = 2.21√h where h = height of aerial or target. Radar waves are bent due to refraction, increasing range by about 15% greater than the geometrical horizon which is 1.92 √h to give 2.21√h. The sea horizon is nm = 2.095√h in meters, so the average person at 3 meters can see about 3.6 nm. The sum of the radar horizon distances of the aerial and target respectively gives the maximum distance at which the target can return an echo. This is then A = 2.21√h (Aerial Height) + B = 2.21√h (Target Height). Superrefraction occurs when warm air is located above cold air masses, and with decreased relative humidity. Sub-refraction can also occur. Radar horizon tables are published in some almanacs and give approximate maximum theoretical radar ranges that can be expected for various radar scanner and target heights.

Radar Horizons

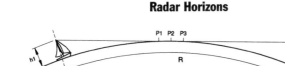

R :DISTANCE
P1 :GEOGRAPHICAL HORIZON
P2 :OPTICAL HORIZON
P3 :RADAR HORIZON

WHERE
R :DISTANCE
h1 :ANTENNA HEIGHT (m)
h2 :TARGET HEIGHT (m)

$$R(nm) = 2.22(\sqrt{h1} + \sqrt{h2})$$

About the Liquid Crystal Displays

LCD displays are now found on most new radars. New generation LCD displays have high resolutions and have good direct daylight viewing qualities. Typically this is 232 x 320 pixels on small displays up to 1280 x 960 pixels on large units. These are either color or monochrome. These displays use the same technology as computer monitors. Essentially the screen consists of many dots, which are called pixels. The status of the pixels is installed in the memory and altered in response to signal processing changes, and is updated each antenna scan. Signal processing uses previous scan and current scan to confirm radar returns, and in many cases it takes 3 scans to display a target at full brightness. This allows clutter to be screened out, and low visibility targets that are within clutter to be distinguished. Unlike the CRT display the rasterscan display is a result of complex digital signal processing of the radar information and allows the use of numerical information on the screen. Digital processing of signals usually has a minimum level that can be displayed, and consequently weak echoes are often rejected. For this reason proper tuning and operation is essential if all targets above that threshold are to be displayed. Manufacturers have introduced a number of processing techniques to overcome these shortcomings.

1. **Single Level Quantization.** This method displays all targets at the same intensity level, regardless of size or strength of return. The main problem is that targets, sea clutter and rain have to be distinguished.

2. **Multi Level Quantization.** This method of processing assigns echoes into strength categories. The stronger echoes appear bright, while weak echoes appear dim on the screen. In these systems inconsistent or weak echoes may not be displayed. These systems are more expensive as more processing power is required.

What are CRT displays?

The cathode ray tube was the primary display type until recent technological advances. The radial display was synchronized with the scanner and effectively displayed every return, the brightness of the target being relative to target strength. These displays were hard to view in daylight. Some new radars still use them, and the images are sharper.

What is chart overlay?

This is a significant technological breakthrough. It enables radar screen images to be directly overlaid onto a chart image. In addition the screen can share images, and windows having chart plotter or fishfinder can be displayed simultaneously. Raymarine uses its HSB data system to allow live transfer of images, and automatic synchronization of chart and radar images is performed.

About radar installation

There are a number of factors affecting the mounting of the scanner on a mast, fly bridge or navigation mast.

1. **Radar Range.** The advantage of increased radar range.

2. **Blind Sectors.** The positioning of the scanner is important. Where scanners are mounted on masts there may be a small forward and stern blind shadow sector.

3. **Scanner Leveling.** On powerboats, in particular planing hull vessels, the scanner has to be mounted with respect to level when on a plane. When stopped the scanner will be angled downwards at the front.

About radar safety and eye damage

Direct exposure to an operating radar transmission can permanently damage retinas or cause blindness. Safe distances are normally given as around 1 meter but recent medical research has recommended an absolute minimum of 2 meters. Scanners mounted very low down where people can pass in front of them represent a very real health hazard, especially with powerful output units.

About radar cable installation

Scanner cables come in a single length and where cutting and joining is required care must be taken. Very few options exist other than multi-pin plugs or junction boxes available for this purpose. Always ensure that radar cables are well protected from chafing where they enter the mast.

How much power does a radar consume?

Small boat radars generally have power consumptions in the range of 3–4 amps. Open scanners typically have a power consumption of 50% greater than enclosed types. This is because they have a heavier scanner and the motor required to rotate it is more powerful.

What is the economy mode?

This function has been incorporated into a number of new radars and is very useful for power conscious boaters. The radar can remain operating with guard zones activated, and the display off to save power. If any target is detected within the guard zone the alarm will sound and display can be called up with one button. With a typical power consumption of 3.3 amps, the power saving mode is only 2 amps, which is quite significant in terms of battery power.

About proper radar grounding

Radar as a transmitter requires proper grounding, and this is usually at the scanner, and the rear of the display unit.

How to operate radar

Correct operation of radar is essential if you are to get the maximum benefit from it. It is prudent to attend a shore-based course as well. Don't be one of the very common radar assisted casualties. At first sight, radar has a bewildering array of controls, but they all have clearly defined functions, which can be easily learned. Many are now automatic and Raymarine calls it Auto GST (Gain, Tune, Sea clutter). Simrad has a useful powerboat function called high-speed mode that doubles antenna rotation speed and therefore image update for high speed target tracking.

Starting up a radar

At power up all radars have a magnetron warm-up period. Upon completion the radar always defaults to stand-by status. When operating a new set, allow it to warm up for at least 30 minutes prior to adjustment and use.

1. **Range Selection.** Always set the range you wish to work on, typically the 12-mile range is the ideal one on the average motorboat given the radar horizon. On a scanner mounted high up a greater range will enable the detection of a large vessel on or just over the horizon. Selection of a range automatically sets the appropriate range ring intervals, the pulse length, and the pulse repetition rate.

2. **Adjust Brilliance.** Adjust the brilliance control to suit your requirements. Do not make it too bright at night, or so dim that targets are not clearly displayed.

3. **Adjust Gain.** Most new radars have automatic adjustment. If manual, adjust the gain control so that screen speckling starts to appear. As this controls the signal amplification, be very careful not to over adjust. Smaller echoes can be masked, or if under the required threshold, they will not appear at all. The gain control is used to remove background noise that appears on the display. Large areas of irregular speckles characterize this across the display. The gain is normally set high for long ranges and reduced for low ones.

4. **Adjust Anti Clutter.** Most new radars have automatic adjustment. This control is often referred to as the sensitivity time constant (STC) control. Clutter is most apparent at the screen center and occurs in that region closest to the vessel. Sea clutter is interference caused by rough seas or wave action where some of the transmitted signal is reflected off the wave faces. Most 3 cm radars transmit a very low signal angle that grazes the water surface. On short ranges, clutter can mask targets, especially weak ones, and the effect decreases at long ranges. Sea clutter always appears stronger on the lee side of the vessel; this is because the vessel heel in that direction exposes the beam to larger water areas, or the backs of passing waves.

5. **Tuning.** The majority of radars are self-tuning, and adjustment will be indicated on a small bar readout on the screen. Most radar can be manually tuned, but this should be done carefully.

6. **Pulse Length Selection.** Pulse length selection is automatic with range changes. At short ranges pulses are at 0.05 microsecond and give better target resolution. At long ranges they increase to 1.0 microsecond.

7. **Pulse Repetition.** Repetition rates vary across ranges from 200 to 2500 per second. Rates determine the size of the area around the vessel where there is a dead zone. At 0.05 microsecond, this is around 150 meters. At 1.0 microsecond this reduces to 30 meters.

8. **FTC. (Fast Time Constant).** Most new radars have automatic adjustment. This control is used to reduce rain clutter. Rain clutter is proportional to the density of the rain,
   fog or snow. Although useful in tracking squalls and rain,
   caution should be used so that targets are not obscured.
   Heavy rain may cause total loss of target definition and
   cannot be adjusted for.

9. **Interference Rejection.** Interference can come from other
   radars operating in the area. This is particularly apparent
   near major shipping routes where powerful commercial
   vessel radars are operating. Use of the IR function will remove these unwanted signals.

All about radar plotting

The whole basis of radar is to detect both stationary and fixed
targets. Radar has a number of basic features to facilitate this:

1. **Range Rings.** The range rings show the radar range and
   will alter with the selected radar range.

2. **Variable Range Maker (VRM).** This function uses the
   range rings and the marker, and many types of radar have
   two VRMs. The readout appears on the screen, but as
   with all navigational exercises, make sure you are meas-
   uring the correct target. Many errors are made this way,
   which is why radar should be used in conjunction with
   other positioning keeping systems, principally the chart
   and Mark I eyeball.

3. **Electronic Bearing Line (EBL).** The most commonly used
   function in conjunction with the VRM enables easy plotting of a target, but be careful, many incidents occur because a bearing was taken without checking what display
   is in use, such as true or relative motion.

4. **Target Expansion.** This function on many types of radar
   allows small or long-range contacts to be expanded, and
   can be very useful when making landfalls of low altitude,
   particularly low atolls and islands.

5. **Off Centering.** A number of radar sets have an offset function. This alters the screen center (the vessel) 50% down
the screen, so that forward long-range observation is possible in the same radar range.

6. **Guard Zones.** The uses of guard zones offer real advantages in safety. Guard zones can be set at a complete cir-
cular coverage or selected for specific sectors. However it
is wrong to rely on these functions. A proper observation
should be made regularly. On some newer radar, an econ-
omy or sleep mode saves power by letting the guard zone
facility and alarm function operating without the screen
being on.

Radar maintenance

There are not much maintenance required on a radar unit, but
undertaking the following will ensure long term reliability:

1. **Connections.** Once every year open the scanner and
tighten all the terminal screws.

2. **Clean Scanners.** Clean the scanner with warm soapy
water to remove salt and dirt. Do not scour or use harsh
detergents.

3. **Scanner Bolts.** Check and tighten the scanner holding
bolts.

4. **Gaskets.** Check that the scanner's watertight gaskets are
in good condition and sealing properly.

5. **Scanner Motor Brushes.** Some scanner motors have
brushes. Check these every six months, manufacturers
sometimes provide a spare set taped to the motor.

6. **Display Unit.** Clean the screen with a clean cloth soaked
with an anti-static agent. Do not use a dry cloth as this
can cause static charging that attracts and accumulates
dust.

Radar troubleshooting

The following gives typical faults on radar that can be investigated and rectified prior to calling a technician.

> **Scanner Stopped:** Motor brush stuck (if fitted); Bearing seized; Scanner motor failure; Scanner motor control failure
>
> **No Display:** Power switched off; Brightness turned down; Fuse failure; Loose power plug; Incorrectly tuned
>
> **Display On, No Targets:** Scanner stopped; Local scanner switch off; Scanner plug not plugged in
>
> **Low Sensitivity:** Ground connection loose; Radome salt encrusted; Open array salt encrusted

About radar reflectors

The subject of radar reflection has been one of continuing controversy over the years with a constant stream of so called reflective safety devices being launched onto unsuspecting boaters. Not to have an effective reflector mounted at all times is, in my judgement, negligent in the extreme. Many motorboats travel at high speeds with significant closing speeds on other motor vessels. There is often little decision making time available and being visible to other vessels is critical. As many larger commercial vessels have ARPA radar that computes and alarms when on collision headings this is also important.

Make sure your vessel can be seen by the big ship radars

I have been on the bridge of fast merchant vessels passing up the English Channel at 24 knots, or through the Caribbean and up the US East Coast dodging motorboats and yachts that are virtually radar invisible. In deep ocean waters, there is still a requirement to be visible. Shipping lanes might imply areas of heavy commercial traffic, but commercial vessels ply waters everywhere. The attitude commonly adopted that no one is keeping a lookout anyway is fatally flawed in its assumptions. Most vessels have the X and S band radars with ARPA collision avoidance tracking and alarm systems, and if the radar cannot lock on to a good consistent signal, the vessel radar cannot compute and track closest approach. Remember, with large and fast vessels, the earlier you are detected, and your course and collision risks assessed, the earlier action can be taken to alter and avoid any close quarters situations.

Radar reflectors help Search and Rescue

Besides the collision risk problem, the important Search and Rescue (SAR) benefits cannot be over stated. It never ceases to amaze me how many SAR operations are called off at night. The amount of valuable flying time and fuel that is expended in aerial search patterns under poor conditions and low cloud bases simply because no effective reflector is hoisted is frightening. All that airborne and seaborne high technology equipment is wasted. Reaction times, rescues and survival prospects even in spite of EPIRBs are decreased in the localization and visual identification phase.

What is the impact of weight and windage?

One of the main reasons stated for not having a reflector hoisted is that reflectors are either too bulky and cause windage, or they are too heavy on a navigation mast in spite of having a radar and lights up there. Firdell has developed compact aesthetically acceptable low profile units specifically for motor vessels.

What about mast shadowing?

Wherever you mount your reflector, there will be some shadowing from the navigation mast. When a reflector such as a Blipper 210-7 is mounted directly to the front of a mast, there is typically a 5–10° blind spot directly aft, the lowest collision risk sector of all. A motorboat's track is far from straight, whether under autopilot or hand steering. Typically variation is in the range of 10° to 25°. Even though some reflective surface will be "seen," this movement will expose a substantial number of reflective corners sufficient to offer a reasonably consistent return at a range of at least 5 miles on a collision course.

How does a radar beam behave?

When a radar beam reaches a target, in theory it reflects back on a reciprocal course to be processed into a range and bearing for display on the screen. In practice, a beam does not simply bounce back off an object, as some materials are more reflective than others, while others absorb the signal.

What are reflective materials?

The best reflective structures are made of steel and aluminum. Materials such as wood and fiberglass do not reflect at all. In fact fiberglass absorbs some 50% of radar signal. There will always be some reflection of most materials, but the direction of the reflected beams will be erratic and very minimal so that no consistent return can be monitored.

About radar reflection consistency

Consistency is one of the major requirements of a good reflector. A good reflector consists of a metallic structure, normally aluminum, with surfaces placed at 90° to each other. If a beam is directed to the center of a re-entrant trihedral, parallel to the centerline, it will reflect around and emerge on a reciprocal course back to the scanner. A re-entrant trihedral is simply a corner with three sides, such as the corner made up of two walls and a ceiling. The basis of understanding radar reflectors comes from a basic principle. The centerline of the corner points in a direction is approximately 36° to each of the sides making up the trihedral. The more the angle increases away from the centerline from a radar beam, the less radar signal returns back.

What are radar reflection standards?

The basic standards include a number of specifications. Never buy a reflector that does not comply. A peak echoing area of 10m^2 is defined as the equivalent to a metal sphere of diameter approximately 12 feet.

The radar reflector types

There are a variety of reflectors on the market.

Octahedral Reflectors. The standard octahedral is a structure consisting of eight re-entrant trihedrals. It was developed in the early 1940s when radar was under development. For optimum effect, they must be mounted in the proper orientation, which is called the "catchrain" position. It is amazing how many are hoisted up by a corner, with one magazine survey having a figure approaching 70%, and my survey closer to 80%. The structure, in fact, has only six effective corners, pointing alternately up and down, the remaining corners being of little use. On the typical 18-inch octahedral polar diagram, the lobes where peak reflection occurs are clearly visible. The peaks clearly exceed the peak echoing area of 10 m^2. The big problem, however, is the big areas between the lobes, where no reflection occurs, or is so minimal that they are under the minimum standards set down by IMO of 2.5 m^2. The total blind spots on the correctly hoisted octahedral total nearly 120°, which is not ideal. The small peaks do not affect the result much. The bad news is, however, that heeled to 15° the blind spots increase to nearly 180°. Signal return can be further decreased where part of the signal, after reflecting of the sea surface, cancels out another beam traveling directly to the reflector. If you are using an octahedral, anything under 18" is a waste of money.

Optimized Arrays Reflectors. The Marconi-Firdell Blipper 210-7 typifies these reflectors. The Blipper consists of an array of precisely positioned re-entrant trihedrals designed to give consistent 360° coverage, and through heel angles up to 30°. As a vessel moves around in a typical three dimensional motion, each of the corners moves in and out of phase to the radar signal, with one corner sending back signal directly, and with others giving partial returns, resulting in a consistent return at all times. The units are rotationally molded inside a radar invisible plastic case, and the windage is only 15% of an 18 inch octahedral, and weighs less than 5 lbs (2 kg). These reflectors have a reputation of meeting and exceeding all published standards, and the numbers mounted on yacht masts attest to this. The Blipper 210-7 has a NATO stock number, which indicates the effectiveness of that unit.

Stacked Array Reflectors. Tubular reflectors that resemble a fluorescent tube or rolling pin typify these reflectors. I have seen boats carrying several. They consist of an array of tiny reflectors housed in a see-through plastic case. These reflector types are purchased on the basis of low cost and small size, not the visibility factor that is the primary requirement. If you sit back and analyze the unit, it is hard to see how the unit can effectively return the amount of signal required. The truth is it can only do so in a near perfect vertical position. At any angle of heel, at 1° or more the unit return falls away to virtually nil. At best tabulated positions, at 0° azimuth, the RCS is 6.05, heeled to 1° it falls to 1.46, and to 0.18 at 2°.

Luneberg Type Reflectors. These devices resemble two half spheres mounted back to back. They are normally fitted to the navigation mast in a fore and aft configuration, but they are very heavy. Of the many criticisms leveled at the reflector, the main ones are that the returned echo was fore and aft but none athwartships, presenting a large and dangerous blind sector, and more importantly the return did not meet the minimum standards of the IMO or RORC having an RCS of around 0.8 m^2 only.

Foil Devices. I have read articles and have heard many people support the concept of hoisting a pair of stockings full of aluminum foil. A case in the UK courts was heard regarding the loss of a catamaran in a collision with a coastal vessel. The skipper did not hoist a reflector because of windage fears reducing sailing performance so he inserted a foil-filled stocking into the mast. The judge in his decision against the catamaran skipper included the following, "To leave an anchorage and proceed without radar into a shipping lane when the visibility is less than 75 yards, so that the navigator is blind, and without a radar reflector so that the boat is invisible, is in my judgement seriously negligent navigation."

What are radar Fresnel zones?

There is an effect in radar where radar signals self cancel, either in the transmission or return path. This problem is related to a variety of factors that includes radar height, target height, sea and earth surface conditions, and radar range. The regions where cancellation occurs are called Fresnel or extinction zones. The regions can be up to a mile in width. In such conditions the radar signal reaching the radar reflector may be relatively weak, with a weak return. The result is no return to the radar, or so weak that it is not processed. It is apparent from the Fresnel tables, that the masthead is not the ideal place to put your reflector, as a relatively large cancellation zone exists. Reflectors are typically mounted at about 4 to 5 meters high.

About radar detectors

These devices are omni-directional units that activate an alarm when radar signal is detected in the vicinity. Typical range is approximately 5 nm. When an alarm is activated, the units can be used as a radar direction finder and a plot of the track of a vessel can be made. The disadvantage is that with more than one fast oncoming vessel, it is difficult to plot all targets and make judgements based on the plot. Vessels may have already made collision avoidance alterations, and this only in the case that a good radar reflector is fitted so that you are radar visible.

What are radar target enhancers?

These are active devices that receive a transmitted radar signal, amplify the signal then re-transmit it back to the source. Unlike passive devices they give good responses around the entire 360° azimuth of the boat. The effective increase in visibility is around 600% ensuring there is a good chance that a ship radar will detect the signal and track it. The Sea-Me device operates on X-band radar signal. The unit also indicates when it is radiated by radar signal. It also has very low power consumption and is easy to mount.

5. AUTOPILOTS

What is an autopilot?

The autopilot is one of those few indispensable electronic items and is often referred to as the non-complaining, non-eating crewmember. The real advances in autopilot technology are powerful microprocessors and equally complex software algorithms that give "intelligent" control. Most autopilot problems occur because of incorrect installation, improper selection, or improper operation, rather than crew personality conflicts. The autopilot consists of a drive mechanism, a heading sensor and the control and power module. The basic function of an autopilot is to steer the vessel on a predetermined and set compass heading or to a GPS position or waypoint. The autopilot then makes course steering corrections proportional to the course error, and will correct to eliminate any overshoot as the course is met. Virtually all autopilots are microprocessor based, and use the proportional rate system of operation. Correction is based on the amount of course deviation and the rate of change.

Warning. Do not use autopilot in any channels, confined areas or heavy traffic zones and also do not use a cellular telephone or handheld VHF as operation can interfere with and cause sudden course changes. There are already several fatalities directly attributable to this.

Motorboat Autopilot System
Courtesy of Vetus

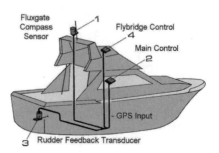

How to select the right autopilot?

The starting point is to look at the manufacturer's recommendations.

1. The steering system installed, which may be wheel hydraulic, wire or direct drive. Also the speed of rudder travel, the rudder size, the required number of turns lock to lock.

2. The loaded vessel displacement, which has wide variations and the beam, draft and displacement. Raymarine recommends that 20% be added to design displacement to get realistic cruising displacement. From experience this is good advice.

3. The type of motoring is also important. For motor cruising you must base all factors on worst weather possible, which means power ratings must be capable of coping with conditions.

How much power consumption?

Always compare the current consumption at full rated load, not average consumption. Many boaters find that the pilot consumes far more power than expected, although much of the heavy power consumption relates to overworking of the pilot. There is no significant difference between average consumptions of all the drive types for a specific vessel size. Power consumption depends on the pilot efficiency and duty cycle, and efficiency factors are typically around 0.5 to 0.8. Factors that directly affect current draw are the force and speed to turn the rudder and the frequency of operation. If you do not have a sailing boat properly trimmed and balanced, or you are carrying too much sail for the weather conditions you may have excessive weather helm which imposes a lot more work on the pilot with greater power consumption. The same applies with excessive yawing in a following sea.

What is autopilot torque?

Torque is the force required to hold the rudder in position due to the pressure of water on the rudder, and to overcome the steering gear resistance of bearings and steering system drives. In many cases this is underestimated, and while the autopilot is fine in light to moderate sea conditions, it often fails to perform in bad weather and to keep a course. Overstressing an autopilot too small for the boat demands generally results in premature failure. The forces that must be considered when selecting an autopilot include the rudder, speed of turns, the speed of the boat through the water and boat weight or displacement. Size ideally requires the maximum turning moment or maximum steering force. The turning moment is the torque applied to the rudderpost needed to turn the boat and is measured in foot/pounds. The steering force is the force needed by the helmsman to steer the boat and the maximum is around 50lbs.

What is the response time?

The response time is very important, and vessels that track well generally have faster response times. Lightweight planing hull vessels that have more rapid heading changes due to the effects of wind, wave and swell require faster response times. The use of gyro-stabilized compasses is often required, such as the KVH azimuth digital gyro compass. The heading data input from an NMEA data sentence is typically around 2–4 seconds and real time inputs are much better at maintaining good response times.

I have a wheel drive!

The rotary drive unit is an integrated gearbox and motor, rotating the wheel via a belt. Vessel steering characteristics can be programmed in to the control system, and a simple clutch lever enables instant changeover to manual steering. The trend in wheel pilots is now towards an enclosed belt drive system. Belts must be correctly tensioned to avoid premature breakage or wear.

I have a linear drive!

The linear drive unit is either an integrated hydraulic ram and pump system or a motor and gearbox drive directly connected to the rudder quadrant.

1. **Advantages.** The linear drive has minimal effect on helm "feel." It is relatively low cost, and the hydraulic units are very reliable. There is also the advantage of a backup steering if some part of the steering drive or pedestal fails. Critical selection criteria are peak thrust, maximum stroke, hard-over times at no-load, hydraulic units are typically up to 12 seconds, and maximum rudder torque, typically up to 3200 Nm.

2. **Power Consumption.** Typical power consumption is relatively low in the range 1.5–3 amps and 2.75–6 amps for larger vessels.

I have a rotary drive!

The rotary drive is usually fitted on vessels where linear drives cannot be installed, or where there are space restrictions, or an inaccessible or small quadrant cannot accommodate any other drive. The motors on these systems consist of an electric motor coupled to a precision manufactured epicyclic gearbox. Some rotary drive units connect to the wheel using chain and sprocket. Power consumption is typically in the range 2–4 amps, and 3–8 amps for larger vessels, and has peak output torques up to around 34 Nm.

I have a hydraulic drive!

The hydraulic drives suit inboard, outboard and stern drive steering systems on powerboats and those sailing yachts with hydraulic steering systems. The hydraulic drive consists of a reversible DC pump unit inserted within the system, or constant running with directional solenoid control valves. Units are rated for maximum stall pressure and peak flow rates, and suit single or double-ended rams.

How to correctly install an autopilot

There are fundamental points to observe when installing autopilots. Always ensure that the drive units are mounted and anchored securely. It is sensible to mount a strong pad at the anchoring points, as it is quite common on fiberglass vessels to see the hull flexing because the inadequate mounting points are unable to take the applied loads.

What about autopilot wiring?

1. **Power Cables.** Ensure that power cables to drive units are rated for maximum current demand and voltage drops, as cable runs are normally long.

2. **Radio Cables.** Make sure that all wiring is routed well away from radio aerial cables, as interference is a major cause of problems during radio transmission. Ensure that a ground cable is run from the computer unit to your RF ground. In rare cases you may have to put on a foil shield to SSB tuner unit interconnecting cables as well.

What about compass installation?

1. **Location in Fiberglass and Timber Vessels.** The fluxgate compass should be installed in an area of least magnetic influence, and close to the center of the boats roll to minimize heeling error. Turning errors can arise if the compass is not properly compensated. The southerly and northerly turning errors increase as distance from the equator increases. This causes slow wandering and slow course correction. Compensation reduces these errors.

2. **Location in Steel Vessels.** Steel vessels pose problems due to the inherent magnetic field in the hull. Raymarine recommends to mount the fluxgate sensor at a minimum of 5 feet above the deck.

3. **Electrical Cables.** Make sure the compass is mounted clear of any cable looms or any other metallic equipment. As fluxgates are invariably installed under bunks do not store any metallic items such as toolboxes or spare parts in the location as often happens.

What about course computer location?

The course computer module should be located well clear of magnetic influences and away from radio aerial cables. While older units were prone to induced interference, newer units are generally made to strict international noise emission standards.

How do the autopilot controls work?

Many adjustments can be made to achieve optimum autopilot operation. The various controls are as follows:

1. **Deadband.** This is the area in which the heading may deviate before the pilot initiates a correction.

2. **Rudder Gain.** This is related to the amount of rudder to be applied for the detected heading error, and must be calibrated. This factor is inextricably linked to proper compass setup and damping. When gain is set too low the correction response is slow to return to set heading. When the gain is too high the course oscillates around the set heading. When excessive gain is used the course is unstable with gradual increases in heading error and course.

Rudder Gain Effects

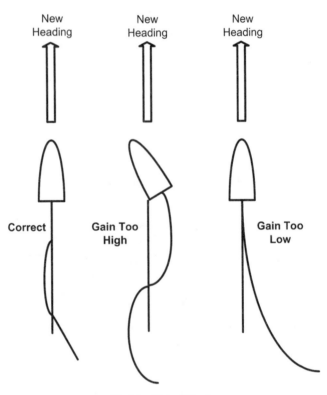

Rudder Gain Effect

3. **Rudder Feedback.** Rudder feedback or reference provides the precise instantaneous rudder position information to the pilot. It is essential that the feedback potentiometer be properly aligned. Most new pilots have a high-resolution potentiometer that offers feedback that is more precise than the coarse units of earlier models.

4. **Rudder Limits.** This controls the limit of rudder travel. The autopilot must stop before reaching the mechanical stops or serious damage may result.

5. **Rudder Damping.** This calibration is used where a feedback transducer is installed and minimizes hunting when the pilot is trying to position the rudder.

6. **Rate of Turn.** The rate of turn limitation is typically 2° per second.

Rate of Turn

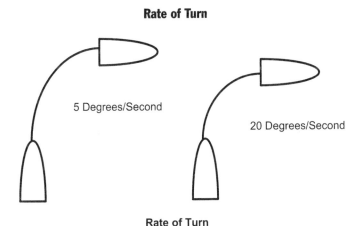

5 Degrees/Second

20 Degrees/Second

Rate of Turn

7. **Dodge and U-Turn Function.** This function usually operates in a 10° step with automatic return to original course, or 180°. The function is useful for dodging containers, debris, etc., or getting out of the way of large ships.

8. **Off Course Alarms.** All autopilots have an off course alarm, which activates when the course heading error exceeds typically 15°. Specific alarm angles can be programmed in.

9. **Auto Trim—Auto Sea State—Auto Wind.** Many of these AutoLearn features for small boat systems were pioneered by Autohelm (Raymarine) and are as follows:

   a. **AutoTrim.** This function automatically compensates for consistent heading errors, such as alterations in weather helm, and applies the correct level of standing helm.

   b. **Auto Sea State.** This function enables the pilot to automatically adapt to changing sea state conditions and vessel responses. It automatically alters the deadband settings, and is controlled by the pilot software. The pilot does not respond to repetitive vessel movements, but only to true course variations.

   c. **Auto Wind.** This function enables the pilot to steer to an apparent wind course. This is usually based on average wind data to account for wind shifts and oscillations and is computed by the course computer.

10. **Magnetic Variation.** The variation must be entered into the autopilot. Many units have automatic compass compensation to correct for errors.

11. **Compass Damping.** The basis for good autopilot performance is proper setting of compass damping. You should start with minimum damping and increase according to conditions. Failure to get this right will cause either lagging or overshooting as rudder is applied to maintain course. This of course has detrimental effects on power consumption rates, as well as making you travel a lot further than you have to. Many lightweight boats may require a rate gyrocompass.

12. **Heading Error Correction.** This correction compensates for northerly and southerly heading errors. Failure to do this will cause amplification of rudder responses on northerly and southerly headings. Raymarine calls this feature AutoAdapt.

About track control

Track control is that function that enables a pilot to steer from waypoint to waypoint in conjunction with a navigation receiver. The autopilot effectively adjusts to take account of tide and current. To do so it takes cross track error (XTE) data and uses it to compute and initiate course changes to maintain the required track.

1. **Limitations.** Most pilots will keep within 300 feet of desired track. Track control is less effective at lower speeds, as tidal stream effect has a greater impact. Differences are noticeable where flow speed exceeds 35% of vessel speed, and careful plotting is essential.

2. **Waypoint Advances.** Many pilots will advance to the next waypoint at a single command. This depends on reception of valid NMEA headers that are the waypoint numbers and bearing to waypoint.

Caution. You must be aware that if a navigation receiver passes incorrect or corrupt position data the pilot may alter course and steer the vessel into danger. Under no circumstances should you use autopilot steering to position or waypoint unsupervised close to the coast or in enclosed waterways. If a large error occurs on a GPS, by the time you realize it, you are aground or worse.

About autopilot interfacing

Interfacing of compasses and navigation receivers is now standard.

1. **Navigation Receivers.** Inputs from GPS enable steering to a position or waypoint. This may be an in-house protocol or NMEA 0183. It is important to remember that position-fixing systems are subject to errors, sometimes extremely large. This will have obvious effects on the steering, so it is important to keep a regular plot, as the autopilot will not be able to recognize the errors.

2. **Fluxgate Compass.** Inputs from fluxgate compass give accurate heading data to course computer.

3. **Rate Gyro (GyroPlus).** These allow rapid real time sensing of vessel yawing prevalent in lightweight vessels in following and quartering seas. This data input supplements the fluxgate signal and allows rapid correction to counter the rapidly altering heading changes that cannot be compensated for by the fluxgate.

How to maintain an autopilot

A number of basic measures can be undertaken to ensure reliability. If you can mount equipment below deck somewhere you will have less problems.

1. **Electronics Temperature.** Keep the electronics modules and processors cool. Manufacturers make units with black plastic to facilitate heat transfer from components inside. While the black casing when exposed to atmosphere may more easily dissipate heat generated inside, equally it absorbs heat. Underrated units that are working hard and under stress will run warm.

2. **Corrosion Control.** Ensure that systems are not exposed to excessive salt water and that seals are intact. Ingress of water is a common failure mode.

3. **Plugs and Sockets.** Regularly check plugs and sockets for water and moisture. Ensure that they seal properly.

4. **Cleaning.** Clean using a damp cloth. Do not use any solvents or abrasive materials. Do not use a high-pressure hose.

How to troubleshoot an autopilot

No Rudder Response: Loss of power; Autopilot fuse failure; Rudder jammed; Plug/connection fault; Control unit fault

Rudder Drives Hard Over: Radio interference (Cell phone/VHF/SSB/Ham); Loss of feedback signal; Rudder limit failure; Fluxgate compass failure; Radio navigation data corruption; Control unit failure

Unstable Wandering Course: Calibration settings incorrect; Over damped compass; Rudder gain setting incorrect; Feedback transducer linkage loose; Control unit fault; Drive unit fault

6. INSTRUMENT SYSTEMS INTERFACING

About instrument systems

The catalyst for the development of the integrated instrument system is undoubtedly the rapid development of microprocessor computing power, electronics miniaturization and appropriate software developments. Another key development is the low cost fluxgate compass. The range of parameters available has now reached more than 75 separate measurements. While discrete instrument systems without the ability to either communicate or calculate anything other than the measured function are available, buyers will probably have to opt for parts of an overall integrated system.

Integrated Instrument System
Courtesy Raymarine

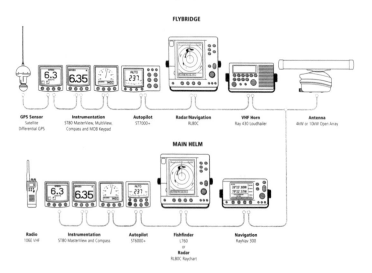

What is integration?

Integration can be simply defined in the context of two principal system capabilities. Integrated systems have a great advantage in that duplication of equipment such as fluxgate sensors, log and depth transducers are eliminated. The two primary system configurations are as follows:

1. All inputs from transducers and information are processed within a single Central Processor Unit (CPU). The information is displayed at the instrument heads and able to communicate freely to external equipment. Data is distributed via a single "daisy chain" network to all instrument heads and connected peripherals such as autopilots and GPS.

2. Total integration where all electronics equipment, which includes the instrumentation, position-fixing systems, autopilot, chart plotters are both physically matched, with a manufacturer specific interfacing protocol. In some cases engine instrumentation and communications are both physically matched as part of that integration process.

What is system architecture?

Basic integrated instrument system architecture varies between manufacturers. The systems in use are as follows:

1. **Discrete Instrument Systems.** These systems have a transducer serving each dedicated instrument head. The head processes and displays the information. Data is exchanged between each instrument on a dedicated network for computation of related data.

2. **Central CPU (Server) Systems.** These systems have a CPU (server) to which all transducers are connected. External data is also connected directly to the CPU. Instrument displays are connected on a daisy chain. The daisy chain interconnecting cable can convey both data in NMEA sentences or using a manufacturer's protocol along with power to each instrument head.

3. **Active Transducer Systems.** The active transducer has a microprocessor incorporated within the transducer, where all raw input data from depth, wind or log is processed. A single cable network interconnects all the transducers with all data being available to any user definable instrument displays. These multifunction displays can be configured with simple keystrokes to display required data.

4. **Wireless Systems.** These award-winning systems from TackTick are solar powered and wireless communications. The data is transmitted from wind and hull sensors to wireless displays. No wiring results in easy installation and complete mobility of the display units.

About interfacing

Interfacing is the process of interconnecting various electronic equipment and systems so that digitally encoded information can be transferred between them and used for processing tasks or display. The manufacturers have to consider the type of physical equipment involved such as connectors and cable, the voltages, impedances, current values and signal timing. At a more technical level, there is the data structure and transfer rate, and the protocol, which determines the information to communicate, the time to communicate, the frequency and error correction. The data messages must also have compatible structures and content. The US National Marine Electronics Association (NMEA) devised the first general digital standard in 1980 (NMEA 0180). This was developed for position-fixing systems to autopilot communication to transfer cross-track error. NMEA 0182, which was for use with plotting systems, followed. The current standard is NMEA 0183, now being slowly replaced by NMEA 2000.

What is NMEA 0183?

This standard was designed to enable transfer of a variety of information between position-fixing systems, radar, compass, plotters and autopilots as well as any other systems either sending or requiring data. NMEA is what is called a single talker, multiple listener architecture. Compliance with the standards is a voluntary one, and there are cases where the implementation of the standards has been technically flawed and communication poor or impossible. The NMEA has standard message sentences. They may be divided into input and transmit sentences, where many are simply transmitted as inputs to processors, while other information is transmitted to appropriate systems or display. Message sentences have the following formats, e.g. HDM = Compass heading, magnetic, WPL = Waypoint Location, XTE = Cross Track Error. There are as many as there are parameters, and listing them all does not serve any practical purpose. One important recommendation was the use of opto-isolation on circuits. The opto-isolator is commonly used in many high noise environments, and an LED and phototransistor are used to provide total electrical or galvanic isolation. This prevents transfer of noise into equipment circuits.

What is NMEA 2000?

The NMEA-2000 interface standard has been developed in conjunction with the International Electrotechnical Commission (IEC). It is a low cost, bi-directional serial data protocol permitting multiple talkers and listeners to share data. It allows GPS, radar, chart displays, sounders, autopilots, engine monitoring and entertainment systems to exchange digital information over a single channel. NMEA-2000 is based on the Controller Area Network Protocol (CAN) originally developed for the auto industry, which is described separately.

What is Raymarine High Speed Bus (HSB)?

These protocols are used for total systems compatibility between all equipment. ArcNet is used as the backbone for the Pathfinder HSB network. The system allows addition of equipment, such as radar, chart plotters, GPS, etc.

What is Furuno NavNet?

This uses an Ethernet 10BaseT (twisted pair) system, which is common in many shore data systems. Systems have a star topology, with each device having a separate set of wires radiating from the hub. When a fault arises it is contained to that one device or cable. Ethernets have high data rates, and cables must be UTP (unshielded twisted pair) standard to ensure data integrity. Make sure cables are routed well clear of fluorescent lights, transformers, etc., to avoid interference.

What is Controller Area Network (CAN)?

This is a fast serial bus designed as an efficient and reliable link between sensors and actuators. CAN utilizes a twisted pair cable for communications at speeds up to 1Mbit/s with up to 40 devices connected. Originally, Bosch developed the electronics standard for automobiles. The system requires an interface for NMEA communications. Features include any node access to the bus when the bus is quiet, and use of 100% of bandwidth without loss of data and automatic error detection, signaling and retries.

What are the other protocols?

1. **SimNet Control.** This is a high speed network protocol used by Simrad instrument systems.

2. **NavBus.** This is the protocol used by NavMan instruments.

3. **B & G Network.** This protocol is also used for total systems communications. NMEA interfaces are provided.

4. **VDO Logic.** This protocol is used for inter-instrument communications, but all instrument heads have an NMEA 0183 output to allow easy connection to other systems.

5. **MagicBus.** This system is based on NMEA 2000 and allows Teleflex Morse systems to communicate multiple engine sensors, actuators and displays.

What causes interface problems?

Virtually all problems with interfacing occur at installation.

1. **Connections.** Unless an equipment manufacturer supplies the interface cable and connector, make sure that the correct pins are used on the output port connector. These vary between equipment and manufacturers. Check with the suppliers, or get them to make up the cable and connector. All connections should observe the correct polarity with respect to ground references. Incorrect connections mean no signals. If the system is fiber optic, ensure the connection is properly inserted, rotate to lock them but do not force them on.

2. **Grounding.** Ensure screens and reference grounds are properly terminated and connected. In many cases data corruption occurs, or it simply does not work.

3. **Set-up.** At commissioning, ensure that the appropriate interface output ports are selected with the correct NMEA or output format selected. In many cases problems are directly attributable to this, and many manuals do not clearly explain the process. In most cases carefully go through the set-up procedures.

4. **Cables.** All cables should be shielded, twisted pair unless stated otherwise. Using other cables may lead to data corruption due to induced noise from adjacent electrical cables and radio transmissions. Flat cables are generally untwisted and round ones are. Use only Cat 3, 4 or 5 with data networks. This is usually 100 ohms impedance and 22 to 26 AWG.

About the various interface cable designations

There are a number of variations in designating interface cable connections. The standard NMEA terminology is signal (positive) and return (negative). NMEA output port variations can be very confusing and obviously lack any real standard notation. Equipment NMEA ports are configured in what is termed a "balanced pair," with both wires carrying the signal. The signal level is the difference in voltage between the pair, and is also known as a differential data signal. The connection of wires is simple, the transmitting device has the transmit connected to the receive port of the other. The receive port is similarly connected to the transmit port of the other. No connections should be made to boat ground or the DC negative.

1. **Data Signal Output:** Data O/P; Tx; Tx hot; A Line; Positive data; Signal O/P; NMEA O/P; NMEA Sig Out; O/P Sig; Data Out; Tx -ve; Tx Data O/P.

2. **Data Return Output:** Gnd; Tx Cold; Ground; Signal Rtn; Return Out; O/P Return; NMEA Rtn; Data Rtn; I/P Gnd; Ref; Negative.

3. **Data Signal Input:** Signal I/P; NMEA Sig In; I/P Sig; NMEA I/P; Rx Data I/P.

4. **Data Return Input:** Signal Return In; Signal Rtn; I/P Rtn; NMEA Rtn; Gnd; Negative; Reference; Ref.

About instrument displays

The ergonomic factors are important and the major decision is whether you want digital, which is the most common, or analog. It is not uncommon to confront a confusing array of digital displays. The aviation and motor vehicle industries have invested heavily in researching easier assimilation of data as primary safety factor; they largely maintain analog presentations.

The Digital Liquid Crystal Display (LCD)

Most displays use a 7-segment display with characteristic chunky numerals. Some displays are difficult to read at wide angles or in bright sunlight, although the new technology is improving things with higher contrasts and wider viewing angles. All units generally have a multi-level backlit illumination system.

About the analog display

The analog display is still seen on some instruments. It is practical on ergonomic grounds as it can make overall instrumentation displays easier to monitor; it is often a needle position or change rather than a value that is monitored. I personally have a preference for analog displays, particularly on depth displays going into coral reefs with the sun behind, they are easier to see. Some manufacturers are incorporating an analog display using the LCD. The LCD Supertwist displays are relatively new; they allow viewing at much wider angles. The CORUS system has a 14-segment display with increased character sizes and improved visibility.

How does a gyro compass work?

The North-seeking action of a gyro is a product of the gyroscope characteristics, the earth's rotation and gravity. In the Simrad Robertson gyro, the gyro rotor is supported inside a horizontal ring on frictionless bearings, and turns at a speed of 12000 rpm. This is supported within a vertical ring, and there is a stabilizer, which generates the North-seeking action. A 24VDC supply is fed to a DC/DC converter for control power to the CPU, and an inverter, which has an output of 3-phase, 100VAC 400Hz. A single-phase 400Hz supply feeds the rotor excitation. The output after processing drives the compass card and output signals for repeaters, radar and autopilot. Prior to starting up the gyro, set the latitude setting for the area of operation. Normal stabilization settling period is up to 4 hours. Check that the compass card of both master and any repeaters are synchronized with panel gyro readings if fitted. Where installed check that panel manual speed setting is correct, and adjust if not. Gyro maintenance consists of daily inspection for abnormal noise, vibration and overheating. When needed, get a change in lubrication oil. The electrical connections should be check tightened yearly. On gyros with digital display, always check for any fault codes that have been generated. These are typically abnormalities in control voltage, rotor speed, servo loop, rotor level and main voltage. Power consumption at 24VDC is 4 amps at starting and 2 amps running. New small vessel systems for large motorboats and trawlers are characterized by the DGS Digital Gyro Compass from KVH which uses a gyro stabilized magnetic sensor. These were developed to overcome the problems of northerly turning errors, and also sudden accelerations experienced during roll, pitch and azimuth in various sea conditions or turning.

What is a fluxgate compass?

A fluxgate sensor detects the earth's magnetic field electronically, sampling hundreds of times per second. The sensing part of the compass consists of coils mounted at right angles in a horizontal plane. Each coil is fed with precisely controlled current subsequently modified by the earth's magnetic field. The processor compares the signals within each coil automatically correcting for variation. The resulting analog output is then converted to digital signals for processing.

What is an electronic compass?

This compass is entirely solid state; the purely electronic sensing overcomes the problems of analog to digital conversion by the output and processing of a digital signal. KVH has developed a compass called GyroTrac. It combines a digital magnetic compass and a three-axis gyro sensor. These compasses meet more demanding requirements of satellite communications and TV systems, ARPA radars and autopilots. When interfaced with GPS, True North is also available. Displays consist of microprocessor-controlled analog rotating cards (450mA), or analog rotating needle (180mA) or digital supertwist LCD (90mA). Power consumption is with lights on. Unlike gyros with long settling times these warm up immediately.

Where to install the sensor

The sensor must be mounted in the area of least magnetic disturbance, so that no interference is induced into it resulting in errors and degrading accuracy. It must also be positioned close to the center of vessel motion, as errors are caused by vessel heeling and pitching. Remember steel vessels pose problems and it must be at least 5 feet above the deck. Accuracy is dependent on proper location clear of interference. Accuracy is typically plus or minus 1 degree although some self compensate to 0.5 degrees, but the display accuracy is still 1 degree.

What is compass damping?

Typically these can be from 5 to 10 levels for some models. The rougher the sea state, the more damping required. A low damping level will result in erratic or rapidly altering headings.

What is compass compensation?

Many have automatic deviation compensation and some will require steering in a circle at commissioning. The compensation takes place with respect to current magnetic deviation. This may vary if you have no electrical devices running, but with everything running accuracy could alter. This will involve re-compensation, which is simple and quick.

All about speed logs

The common paddlewheel has magnets imbedded in the wheel blades, and a detector giving a pulse that can be counted and processed. Earlier units had a glass reed switch that was prone to impact induced mechanical failure; new units have a Hall effect device. The signal pulses are normally seen as a voltage change, such as zero and five volts, to give a stepped characteristic that can be counted. The result is directly proportional to the speed and distance traveled. Counting may be either the pulses per second or based on pulse length, proportional to distance.

Log Transducers

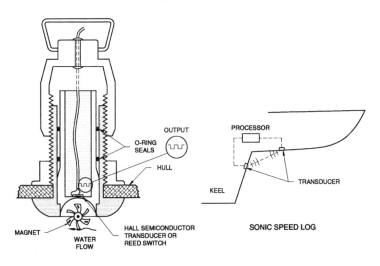

PADDLEWHEEL LOG

SONIC SPEED LOG

About ultrasonic logs

B & G, Echopilot and Kaytek have sonic speed sensors, which are significantly more accurate with near linear outputs. The transducer consists of two 2 MHz piezo electric crystals. These transmit short pulse acoustic signals simultaneously and reflect the signals off water particles approximately 6" away, clear of the turbulent boundary layer. The water particles pass through the forward then the aft beam, and the transmission time of the acoustic sound signal between the two crystals is then measured. The time delay is used to determine precise speed based on the known distance between the two transducers.

About speed log installation

Correct installation is essential if the log is to be accurate and reliable. Observe the following notes:

1. **Location.** The log transducer is normally mounted in the forward third of the hull, and must be in an area of minimal turbulence, called the boundary layer.

2. **Cabling.** Do not run depth sounder and log cables together as interference may result.

About log calibration

Log calibration normally requires the use of a measured mile. Many new logs are self-calibrating or have an optional manual calibration. The calibration run should be carried out at slack water and calm, windfree conditions to prevent any inaccuracy. Prior to making a run, check that the correct magnetic course has been worked out to ensure the vessel takes the correct course, and this means making appropriate corrections for variation and compass deviation. Make the runs under power at a constant engine throttle setting. Ensure that transits used are accurately observed at the start and finish of each run. The formula for determining the log error is as follows:

1. Runs 1 & 2 (ground measurement) = Correction K

   Runs 2 & 2 through water

2. The resulting figure will show either under or over reading, and this is used either to calibrate log or correct readings.

Transducer maintenance

Logs in general need little maintenance, except for paddlewheels.

1. Remove and check the paddlewheel for smooth, frictionless rotation. Apply some light oil to the spindle.

2. Check that the O-ring seals are in good condition to prevent leakage into the bilge.

Transducer troubleshooting

To test whether the paddlewheel transducer or the instrument head is faulty:

1. Disconnect the log input cables to the instrument head or processor.

2. Use a small piece of wire, rapidly short out the terminals and observe whether a reading is indicated. If there is, the transducer is faulty. If there is nothing, the instrument head is probably at fault.

About wind instruments

The typical wind system comprises an integral wind speed and direction unit along with instrument head.

1. **Wind Speed.** The anemometer is essentially a rotating pulse counter, similar to the log. The pulses are counted and processed to give speed.

2. **Wind Direction.** This part of the masthead unit consists of a simple windvane, with a number of methods used to measure the angle and transmit the signals to the instrument head or processor. Some units use an electromagnetic sensing system. Other units use an optical sensing system to identify coded markings that relate to the windvane direction.

    a. Apparent Wind Direction. The measured wind direction is apparent wind, which indicates angle relative to boat speed.

    b. True Wind Direction. The true wind data is a result of the instrument processing vessel course, speed, apparent wind direction and speed.

Transducer installation

The transducer is mounted on the signal mast above the radar and navigation lights.

1. **Fastening.** It is important that the unit is properly fastened down, especially as transducer units are installed into a simple bracket assembly and are removable in many cases. Ensure fore and aft alignment is correct to reduce inaccuracies in angle readings. Birds and lightning are the main cause of damage, followed by vibration.

2. **Electrical Connections.** Make sure that the cable connector is securely fastened. It is good practice to put a few wraps of self-amalgamating tape around it to prevent ingress of water. If you apply petroleum jelly or silicon grease do not fill the socket, as it is pushed in with the transducer unit and contributes to a poor electrical contact. Keep the electrical connections dry and tape as suggested. Apply grease to the screw threads to minimize seizing.

Transducer maintenance

There are few tasks and the following should be checked every six months or before the start and the end of the season:

1. Check securing bolts and frame, and tighten as required.

2. Check cable connector for ingress of moisture and water, as well as for signs of corrosion on the pins. Smear a small amount of petroleum jelly or silicon grease around the threads when replacing it, and rewrap with self-amalgamating tape. Ensure that the cable is not chafing at any access point.

3. Check that the anemometer rotates freely without binding or making any noises that indicate bearing seizure or failure. Check that the cups are not split or damaged, as this frequently occurs with birds.

4. Apply a few drops of the manufacturer's light oil into the lubrication hole, and rotate freely to ensure that it penetrates the bearing.

5. Make sure that the connections in the junction box are tight and there is no corrosion of cable or screw connectors.

Instrument installation

The following should be observed when installing an instrument system:

1. **CPU Location.** Always install the CPU or data box if one is used, in a clean, dry area that enables easy access for transducer cables. Ensure that the CPU unit is mounted well away from fluxgate compasses, LORAN, GPS receivers, VHF and SSB radios, satellite radomes, AM/FM radios and cellular phone aerials. The CPU must be a minimum one meter from a magnetic compass.

2. **Transducer Cables.** Transducer cables should not be lengthened or shortened, coil up the extra length at the transducer end.

3. **Instrument Covers.** Do not cover or mount your instruments behind clear plastic covers. This has the effect of magnifying the heat from the sun and burning out the instruments. Always use the covers provided when not in use to prevent UV damage and weathering.

4. **Cables.** Avoid cable stresses and ensure that cables are not bent sharply. All cables must be taken through proper deck transits to connection boxes. Always run cables well away from radio antennas and heavy current carrying cables.

Instrument maintenance

1. **Check Connections.** Bad electrical connections are the source of many failures, as is the ingress of moisture into connection boxes and plugs. When a short circuit occurs, the spike that is generated often causes a failure in the electronics. Ensure that all boxes are dry, well waterproofed and connections tight.

2. **Remove Transducers.** Where possible always remove log or depth transducer while at a mooring or in port and replace with the dummy. Always ensure the paddle rotates freely and is clear of any growth.

Instrument troubleshooting

No Display; Loss of power; Cable connection fault; Instrument fault

Partial Display: Processor fault; LCD fault; Transducer fault

Erratic Readings: Connection degradation; Interference from radios, electrical, etc.; Low battery voltage; Transducer fault

No or Low Boat Speed: Transducer not installed; Transducer not connected; Fouled transducer; Transducer misaligned; Paddlewheel seizing

High Boat Speed: Electrical interference

No Wind Speed: Mast base connection fault; Mast head unit plug fault; Anemometer seized; Mast head unit fault; Processor fault; Low battery voltage

Erratic Wind Angle: Loose connections; Corroded mast head unit plug; Water in mast head unit plug; Mast head unit fault

No Depth Indication: Transducer damaged; Transducer fouled; Low battery voltage

Intermittent Shallow Indication: Weed or fish: Water aeration

Shallow Readings in Deep Water: Check your charts! Outside depth range

Inconsistent Depth Readings: Muddy or silted bottom; Low battery voltage; Poor transducer interface (in hull only)

7. NOISE AND INTERFERENCE

About interference

Interference is the major enemy of electronics systems, corrupting position fixes and causing general performance problems. It is often the cause of electronics damage. Interference and noise superimpose a disturbance or voltage transient onto power or signal lines and this corrupts or degrades the processed data. The following describes problems and some solutions.

About voltage transients

The voltage transient is the most damaging and comes from many sources. The best known is the corruption of GPS and LORAN data where the power is taken off an engine starting battery. If a significant load is applied, there is a momentary voltage drop (brown out condition), followed by an increase. This under-voltage disturbance can exceed 100 volts in some cases, damaging power supplies, wiping memories or corrupting data. The same applies to two battery systems where the house bank supplies items such as electric toilets and large current equipment. A starting battery voltage can have a 3–4 volt dip on starting. Transients are also caused by the variation or interruption of current in the equipment power conductor.

What is induced interference?

Electrical fields are radiated from cables and equipment and this is induced into other nearby cables or equipment. The most common causes of this are cables running parallel or within the same cable bundle, and it is also called mutual coupling. Always run power supply cables and data cables separately and make sure the cables cross at 90°. In particular run power cables to sensitive equipment separate to main power cables to reduce inductive and capacitive coupling to signal conductors.

About noise sources

There are a number of noise sources on motorboats. Noises can be classified as Radio Frequency Interference (RFI) or Electromagnetic Interference (EMI). Noise also occurs in differing frequency ranges, and similarly equipment may only be prone to problems within a particular frequency range. Multiple noise sources can cause a gradual degradation of electronics components and when the cumulative effects reach a certain point the devices fail.

What causes arcing noise?

These are repetitive spikes that are caused by commutators and sparking of brushes. The brushes on any alternator, particularly if dirty, can cause sparking and noise. Charging systems and loose connections are usually responsible for this. The most common cause is loose or poor engine return paths for alternators, when the negative path arcs across points of poor electrical contact. This is also caused by ignition systems from distributors and spark plugs being impressed on a DC system, often through radiation to adjacent cables.

What causes induced coupling interference?

Wiring that is installed in parallel with others can suffer from inductive coupling interference. This is like a transformer with a single turn primary and secondary coil, with the magnetic effects causing the induction. Low ground impedances and unbalanced circuits are the most probe, with serial data, multi-cable control and co-axial cables being the most susceptible ones.

What is capacitive coupling interference?

This is most common in high frequency circuits and in high impedance to ground circuits such as balanced pair systems.

What is ripple noise?

Ripple is created in any rectifier bridges (diode, SCR etc) such as alternators, chargers, fluorescent lights and inverters. It is usually a high-pitched whine. Good equipment has suppressed electronics. Ripple badly degrades communications audio quality.

What about static charges?

1. **External Charges.** This type of interference can arise due to static build-up in rigging. On reaching a certain voltage level, the static discharges to the ground, causing interference. Another common cause is when dry, offshore winds occur, and a static charge builds up on fiberglass decks. The problem is prevalent on larger fiberglass vessels with large deck areas. A lightning protection system can ground out these charges.

2. **Engine and Shaft Charges.** This type of interference can arise due to static build-up both induced and due to moving parts in the engine. The static discharges to ground and causes interference. Shaft interference can arise due to static build-up on propeller shafts. The static will discharge to ground when it reaches a high voltage level, and cause interference. Typical cures are grounding of the shaft with a brush system.

What is surge or electromagnetic pulse?

This can be caused by lightning activity, and pulses can be induced into electrical wiring and aerials. The allowable surge is 100 volts for 50ms and 70 V for 100ms.

What are spikes?

Turn-on spikes result from the initial charging of power supply input filters on power supplies. Turn-off spikes arise when reactive loads are switched, and the magnetic fields collapse on inductive loads, such as transformers, relay or contactor coils, solenoid coils, pump motors, etc. Spikes can be as much as 500V peak-to-peak. MOV suppressors are often put across the coils.

About noise suppression methods

There are a number of methods that can be used to reduce or hopefully eliminate interference. The use of shielded cables along with proper grounding is important, but the use of proper equipment enclosures is also critical, as this minimizes electromagnetic radiation.

1. **Filters.** A filter or capacitor is installed close to the noisy equipment, and effectively short circuits noise in the protected frequency range. Filters may take a number of forms. The filter consists of either a capacitor, or a combination of capacitor and inductor connected across the power supply lines. STO-P uses filters with very low ground impedances, typically lower than 20 milliohms at 1kHz, which cleans out ripple. An option is to supply sensitive equipment through a Navpac from NewMar. This is a supply-conditioning module that filters out spikes and noise, regulates supply voltage, and has an internal power pack to ensure supply continuity. The Start-Guard from NewMar also protects against the surges that occur when the voltage drops when starting engines. This device is connected in parallel with the equipment, and sense circuit is connected with the starter switch or solenoid. The internal battery supplies the load when starting and recharges when in standby mode. The units are rated at 20 amps.

2. **Suppressors.** Suppression modules from Charles Marine use MOV technology and are available in AC and DC types. Many alternators do not have these fitted, so install them. Normally you will have noticed radio noise or interference on electronics equipment. A 1.0-microfarad is a starting point, but even experimentation with a couple of automotive types is simple and inexpensive.

3. **Ferrite Chokes.** Ferrites chokes are sleeves or rings that are placed over cables. They allow differential mode signals through but block common mode currents by interrupting RF ground loops and prevent RF from coupling into the cables. They are ideal for eliminating problems in e-mail connections to notebook, HF modem and SSB connections and are recommended by SailMail in their installations. They can also be used on any cables such as autopilot cables or others exposed to interference. The Fair-rite chokes are available in the US from Newark Electronics (800-639-2759) and Amidon Electronics (714-850-4660). It is important that when clipping on ferrites no air gaps are left between the ferrite halves. Co-axial ferrite line isolators such as the T4 are available from Radio Works (www.radioworks.com) and are used on the coaxial cable and placed on near the tuner unit. These block the stray RF ground path from the coaxial shield and transceiver grounds.

Power system stabilization

In cases of high voltage induction it is necessary to clamp voltages to a safe level, typically around 40 volts. One of the major causes of lightning strike damage is the failure of equipment power supplies to cope with high voltage transients. The most common method of achieving this is to connect a metal oxide varistor (MOV) across the power supply. As the voltage rises the resistance alters to shunt the excess voltage. A second method is the use of an avalanche diode across the supply. MOVs are designed for AC systems, and DC surges tend to have longer time durations. Also MOVs can be blown without warning.

All about interference and noise screening

Screening is used to mask sensitive equipment from radiated interference. Common sources include radio equipment and high current carrying cables. The equipment or cables are covered and grounded by metal covers or screens (commonly called the Faraday cage). This may be a simple aluminum cover grounded to the RF ground point.

1. **Equipment Covering.** A useful product is the Sonarshield conductive plastic sheet. Simply cover the Loran, GPS, radar or radio casing (Southwall Technologies, 1029 Corporation Way, Palo Alto, CA 94303). The total metal Faraday shield approach is rarely required.

2. **Cable Covering.** Noisy power cables can be wrapped in noise tape, which is a flexible copper foil with an adhesive backing such as that from NewMar. I have used this product and method.

3. **Cable Shields.** Shields are designed to protect against interference from unknown or unspecified sources. The effectiveness of shields is measured in terms of transfer impedance. This is a measure of effectiveness in capturing the interference field and preventing it from reaching the conductor pairs inside. Data cables have shields made from a foil/polymer laminate tape or layers of braiding. These also may have a drain wire installed to enable termination of the screen. Most manufacturers will also specify the termination of shields. Never ground at both ends, always ground one end only, typically the equipment end. In many cases shields are not connected at all, so check and connect them.

4. **Grounding.** The ground must be clean, which means that it should have a ground potential between equipment no greater than 1 volt peak-to-peak. A ground is capable of also conducting transients and emissions so it must be sound. Another grounding source on boats is the grounding of static causing equipment such as shafts and engine blocks. As discussed in alternators, the negative connections

to the engine block are a common source of problems. Ensure that the starter motor negative is attached close to the starter itself. Add an additional negative to the alternator. In many cases, interference is caused by arcing and sparking within the engine, as it is effectively part of the negative return conductor. Modifying the negative system eliminates this problem. Ensure that all ground connections are clean and tight.

5. **Cancellation.** The wires to a piece of equipment can be twisted together. This effectively causes cancellation as the electrical fields are reversed.

How to troubleshoot noise

Tracing the sources of noise is a matter of logic and systematic switching off the equipment to find the source. In some cases it may consist of two or more sources causing a cumulative effect. Some noise will be simply intermittent, such as static discharges, which may be synchronized with hot dry wind conditions, or lightning pulses, which may not even be visible locally. A cheap battery powered AM radio is a good tool for tracking down radiated sources on board, with static being easily picked up. Passing it close to equipment is the method used. Some noise is simply related to time of day. There is also interference from ionosphere factors on radios. GPS, HF, and satellite communications may all be affected simultaneously, giving the appearance of some greater problem.

About cable routing and noise

Cable planning is a major cause of problems. If you have problems cable routing will have to be assessed and possibly require re-routing of the sensitive cables.

8. SECURITY AND SAFETY SYSTEMS

Fire detection systems

Smaller boats should invest in self-contained units that have an integral battery. Larger vessels may have sophisticated, analog addressable, multi-zone fire systems installed. The control unit processes sensor information and allows the setting of alarm thresholds, and time delays that activate alarms. The sensors or transducers are the detectors and manual call points that are processed. The sensors output analog signals, which are compared with fixed levels in the controller. The controller software program also utilizes processing algorithms when using two or more separate alarms to decide on alarm activation, or to vary threshold compensation for aging or dirt accumulations, which tend to cause nuisance false alarms. A fire system has a combination of sensor types that cover various fire types, risks and characteristics. It is important that you read and understand the technical manual for your own system, with operational, test and maintenance requirements. Some fire suppression systems also are interfaced with an automatic diesel engine shutdown system, which stops the engine when the extinguisher is activated.

All about smoke detectors

These are installed in most locations, and modern centralized systems have addressable sensors. Smoke detectors must be located so that the thermal convection of smoke carries to the detector. The various smoke detectors are described and suit various fire types, as this affects the response time of each. The various types are different depending on the size of the smoke particles. Hot fires tend to have very small and almost invisible particles; low temperature smoldering fires will have larger visible particles. Ion chamber detectors react quickly to small particles, but are slower on larger particles, and the reverse is true for photoelectric detectors. Aerosol smoke detector testers are used to check units, test notes should be observed.

1. **Optical Smoke Sensors.** These detectors are ideal for low levels of smoke. The Raleigh forward scatter principle uses the scattering properties of light from smoke particulates when they enter a light beam. Units are designed not to be activated by insects and background airborne dust particles. Test response time is 6 to 22 seconds.

2. **Ion Chamber Detectors.** These operate by the air within a chamber being ionized by a very small radioactive source of Americium 241. This allows a small current to flow between the source and a cover, which has a fixed voltage between them. The units operate best with invisible smoke materials released by fast burning fires. Test response time is 6 to 12 seconds.

3. **Heat Sensors.** There are two types, the first activates when a set temperature is reached; the second activates based on the rate of temperature rise above a threshold level. Many units combine both functions. The heat sensor uses a bridge consisting of two matched thermistors, which are arranged to respond on absolute temperature and rate of temperature change, and are fed to a differential amplifier. The thermistors are negative temperature coefficient types, one is exposed to air and the other is within the detector casing. The bridge voltage will track constant temperatures; when the temperature changes rapidly, the sense thermistor will be unable to follow, and generates an analog output.

About carbon monoxide sensors

These operate on the principle of oxidation of carbon monoxide gas to carbon dioxide. This conversion process takes place within a catalytic sensing cell. The process requires an exchange of electrons and the flow of electrons generates a small current within the cell. These are suited to slow burning fires. The 0–20mA output is normal at 7.5mA; when the carbon monoxide level increases a proportional output is also generated, and the alarm is activated before reaching the limit of 50ppm.

Maintenance and troubleshooting

All fire systems must be checked regularly to ensure proper and reliable detection and alarm functions. Automatic extinguishing systems (CO2) must be disabled when testing, along with automatic closing fire dampers or ventilation shutdowns. If a detector does not respond after 60 seconds, it is probably faulty.

    a. **Weekly Checks.** Check the controller unit for line faults and any visual and audible alarms; also, check one detector or manual call point within each zone. The control unit internal alarm and indicators should operate. The alarms around the boat also should function. Check internal standby batteries.

    b. **Every 3 Months.** Simulate a fault by removing a detector from a base. Check all sensors for physical damage, look for paint, grease and dirt. Do not open or attempt to clean ion chamber units, they must be returned to the supplier using radioactive materials handling precautions. Check the internal standby batteries.

    c. **Annually.** Check and tighten all control unit terminals. Check all cables, connectors and mountings. Test all sensors, detectors and call points. Internal standby batteries usually require replacement every 3 to 4 years.

All about gas detection

Any gas is potentially lethal on a boat, either LPG, CNG or other. Leaking gas accumulates in the lowest point, which is the bilge. It only requires a small amount of gas (about a cupful) to completely destroy the vessel if ignited. If gas is installed, a quality gas detector is essential. All flammable gases have a lower explosion limit (LEL). As long as the gas/air ratio remains within this range no explosion can occur. Once this level is exceeded, a significant risk of explosion exists. A gas detector must detect gas concentrations before the limit is exceeded, typically 50% LEL. Better units have a sensitivity of 25% LEL.

What are the detector types?

Two types of gas detectors are in use in detection systems.

1. The main commercial sensor is the catalytic type. On off-shore installations, these are recalibrated on a weekly basis to ensure precise operation.

2. The most common type of sensor on small vessel detection systems is the semi-conductor type, which consists of a sintered tin oxide element. On detection of gas, the resistance alters activating the alarm circuit. It must be remembered that it takes several days of operation before the sensor stabilizes, and final calibration can be made. Detectors may be subject to temperature drift in the sensing circuit and good detectors incorporate a temperature sensor to correct this and ensure accuracy.

3. Other well-known devices use what is called the pellister principle. These devices consist of two heated platinum wire elements. One is coated with gas detecting material; the other is used for temperature and humidity compensation.

About proper detector installation

Sensor elements must be mounted in the areas where gas may accumulate. The problem is of course that bilge water or moist salt air can contaminate the element causing degradation and failure to detect.

1. **Testing.** In testing, ideally a precise gas/air mix of the appropriate LEL ratio is used to calibrate the alarm level. In practice however this is never done. The simplest method to test whether the system functions is by activating a gas cigarette lighter or even a disposable lighter at the sensor. Activation should be almost immediate.

2. **Alarm Outputs.** All detectors should have a gas bottle solenoid interlock. If gas is detected, the solenoid should be closed. This function should be fail safe in operation. An external alarm can be connected, or activate a fan.

All about troubleshooting alarms

The following important factors regarding troubleshooting should be noted:

1. **Alarms.** If an alarm goes off assume it is real. If the alarm is proven to be false, you can normally readjust the alarm threshold, but do so only enough to compensate for the sensor drift causing the nuisance activation.

2. **Sensor Element.** The principal cause of problems is invariably the sensor element degrading. It is wise to carry a spare sensor for replacement. If after replacing the sensor the alarm still causes problems, have the electronic unit tested.

All about boat security systems

Keeping the villains out of the boat is always a challenge. You can never keep out a determined thief, but my attitude is always to make the exercise as difficult, uncertain and unpredictable as possible. A variety and combination of detectors and sensors can be coupled with control units and alarms, including:

1. **Ultra-sonic Sensors.** These types of sensors are generally unsuited to vessel installation, as they are set off too easily by spurious signals, and they have relatively high power consumption.

2. **Microwave Sensors.** These are often combined with PIR and use short K-band to reduce false alarm rates.

3. **Infrared.** Passive InfraRed (PIR) sensors direct a pattern of infrared beams over a set area. When a heat source is detected, the alarm is activated. Some PIR units use pattern recognition to screen out pets. Only one unit properly located is required to cover a typical saloon, but the installation sight must be carefully selected so that it is not easily visible. There are also infrared beam detectors. They have relatively low power consumption.

4. **Proximity Switches.** Magnetic switches are used on hatches and access points and hard wired to the control unit. The magnetic reed switches are N.O. SPST (Normally Open Single Pole Single Throw). The advantages are that the alarm is activated before a thief has broken in or entered the boat, so that an alarm will catch him on deck or in view.

5. **Pressure Pads.** Pressure-activated pads require installation under carpets and mats. They have a 2 wire N.O. SPST circuit. They can also be placed under a rubber mat in the cockpit to alarm or activate lights before entry.

Security System

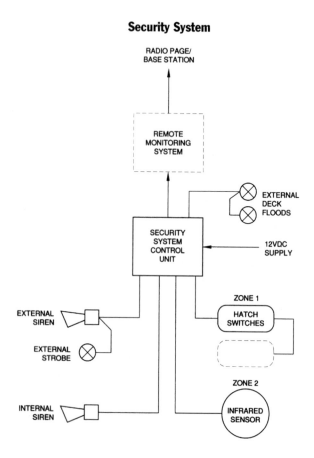

About CCTV surveillance systems

Many larger boats have installed CCTV systems. Cameras need to be properly located for maximum benefit. The camera site must ensure there are no blind spots, and be relatively hard to tamper with. Cameras must also be adapted to the environment, outside units having robust and corrosion resistant housings. External units may also have wash and wipe facilities. Units within machinery spaces must be mounted to avoid vibration and excessive heat. Average power consumption is 4 watts plus the monitor.

About camera systems

Systems consist of the cameras, both color and monochrome. Monochrome (black and white) cameras use charged coupled device (CCD) image chips, with good resolution in low light conditions. Simple units can have a simple F-stop adjustment with manual or auto iris functions for variable light condition adjustments and field of view selection. Systems also have TV monitors, pan and tilt control panels and sequential switcher units including Quad splitter units to either sequentially show multi-camera images, or simultaneously show images from four cameras.

About camera control

Camera controls should be checked. The auto Iris on zoom lenses should be checked in all light conditions, and if an override facility is installed, check control manually. Check that all cables and connectors are secure. Switching units such as Quad units that split 4 camera images to a monitor screen should be checked. Problems are uncommon, and are limited to power supplies, operator programming errors, or inputs from a specific camera, usually a cable connection.

About CCTV camera maintenance

Regular cleaning of the glass and refilling of washer reservoirs is required. Do not operate wipers on a dry glass, as scratching and scoring of the glass by hard salt crystals will affect image quality. Cold climates will require automotive grade antifreeze screen washer liquids. The pan and tilt facility should be operated through the entire azimuth range and complete up and down movement. Any vibration and jerking movements will indicate seizing, or fouling of camera housing. All fastening bolts and screws should be checked and tightened each year. Cables should be examined for damage and degradation. Wiper blades if fitted should be replaced. If housings are removed check the seals and replace if perished.

Security alarm indication systems

Once an alarm is triggered various systems may be activated to indicate the presence of the intruder.

1. **Strobe Light.** The mounting of a high intensity Xenon strobe light on a high location for maximum visibility is the most common indication method. Many install a blue light, but you simply cannot see it easily, which is why police forces worldwide now use a red/blue/white light combination on vehicles.

2. **Audible Alarm.** Install the highest two-tone output siren that is available. Install one outside, and one inside. A high decibel output unit inside can be very painful to an intruder, and simply cut short his stay. Several different alarm signals can panic or disorientate the thief.

About security interlocking systems

The interlocking of various systems to the alarm is another popular method:

1. Deck and foredeck spotlights, as well as any lights on masts and fly bridges can be interlocked to come on with alarm activation.

2. Mobile phone dial-out and pager. These options automatically dial out to nominated pagers and cell phones.

3. GPS Tracking. This is an autodialing system with a prerecorded message via the GSM phone and allows PC based tracking. Global coverage uses Inmarsat.

4. Camera Systems. These can be small discrete CCD low light cameras, or vandal proof pan and tilt color cameras. They can be coupled to a video recorder.

5. Volvo has an electronic immobilizer that shuts off the engine fuel feed for those intent on stealing the boat.

About time delays

Alarm activation always has both entry and exit delays. Once the alarm is activated you have to get out, and when you enter you need time to isolate the alarm. I prefer to fit a remote isolator hidden in a locker, and have virtually minimal delay. Legally you may have to ensure that there is a reset function. Generally, the law restricts operation for ten minutes, and then alarms must cease. A popular method of really ambitious thieves is to set off the alarm and come back when the silence returns, so make sure that it is an auto reset type.

What are back to base alarms?

This method of alarm monitoring transmits an alarm via radio signal back to a 24-hour monitoring station for action, either at the marina or off site. These systems incorporate total vessel alarm monitoring, which includes bilge levels, smoke and fire detection, gas detection and security. You can do this via Internet to your own home computer if you wish.

Additional anti-theft precautions

These additional steps also help deter thieves. Place clear notices at all access points, stating that the vessel is protected by alarms. Place an outside alarm in the cockpit. Hide valuables and keep curtains drawn. Put a light and radio on a time switch, with a few variable times, not just the same time every evening.

9. ENTERTAINMENT SYSTEMS

About satellite TV

There are some very sophisticated TV systems available including Applied Satellite Technology (AST); KVH TracVision and SeaTel. Systems operate on the C-Band (3.7–4.2 GHz) and the Ku-Band (10.7–12.95 GHz), and some are dual frequency. The units use a control unit, and auto-tracking gyro-stabilized antenna dishes housed in a radome. Radomes have sizes in the range 0.6–1.5m. As satellite tracking has to be fast and accurate to remain locked on, units also have pitch and roll sensors, with 3-axis servos and track satellites while compensating for vessel pitch, roll and yaw. These sensors use rate gyro sensors and inclinometers. Some units also have integral GPS receivers that supplement the NMEA gyro data. With the power on, typical satellite acquisition times are around 5 minutes. There are several search modes including auto, manual, search and scan modes. The servo is normally a high torque brushless motor. Installation principles are virtually the same as for Inmarsat antennas. As satellites transmit to limited areas reception is dependent on being within the footprint. Footprints are generally limited to coastal and landmass areas, and proper selection of the correct tracking frequency is necessary. Power consumption is typically 3–5 amps. There are over 300 TV channels available in Europe and many more in the US and elsewhere. CD quality music and high speed Internet downlinks are available.

Maintenance and troubleshooting

Systems should be inspected on a routine basis, with the system switched off and isolated. Visually inspect cables for chafing or damage. Radome interiors should be checked for water ingress and corrosion. All nuts and bolts should be checked and tightened. Some units have desiccant cartridges and these should be replaced if saturated. Faults are usually due to incorrect setup, satellite acquisition problems, or wrong satellite selection. Systems also have comprehensive monitoring and menu based systems, and reading the manuals is important.

Television

There are a range of TVs that are designed for 12- and 24-volt operation. For long distance passage makers multi-system units with NSTC and PAL reception are available. Television aerials and their performance on vessels is a controversial subject along with often over-optimistic performance claims by some manufacturers. They are also relatively expensive. Comparable performance with home aerials should not be expected, and attempting to get a reasonable picture while under way is generally out of the question, and the off-watch should stick to DVDs and videos. The principal problem is getting a good picture at anchorages, without the continual ghosting that occurs in varying degrees of severity as you swing around. The ghosting problem largely depends on the path of the transmitted signal, and the frequency characteristics of the transmission.

About signal distortion

Transmission signals are essentially straight line and do not bend significantly when meeting obstructions. The effect is one of creating shadows and areas of low signal behind the obstruction. Reflection of the signal also alters the direction of propagation causing signals to arrive at the aerial from a direction other than the straight-line path from the transmitter. The receiver ultimately receives two signals that arrive at times different to each other. The effect is the reception of a distorted signal pattern. The distortion of signal occurs from a number of sources that include hills, other boats, rigging and reflection off the water surface. Signal transmissions are generally horizontally polarized. When signal is reflected, the polarization is altered, causing distortion. The variety of TV transmission systems in use is confusing. The main systems are M/NTSC (US, Canada, Guam, most of South America); B.G/PAL (Australia, Netherlands, Spain, Portugal, Italy, Canary Islands); I/PAL (UK, South Africa); L/SECAM (France).

About boat TV aerials

1. **Directional Aerials.** These aerials can be aligned with the transmitted signal. Aerials are of the domestic type, and may be of use if you live on board and rarely venture out from the marina, but on an anchorage they are useless, as you must continually adjust the aerial.

2. **Omni-directional Aerials.** These aerials are able to receive transmission signals consistently and are not affected by the vessel swinging at anchor or mooring. This type of aerial does not discriminate between directly transmitted or reflected signals. The most common type of aerial is a ring or loop, which is hoisted when required. These aerials do have a problem with reception of reflected signal from any masts and rigging, and perform poorly in marinas where there are many other vessels tied up.

3. **Active Aerials.** These units are typically a fiberglass or plastic dome, with an integral omni-directional loop aerial element inside. The signal is amplified to compensate for the smaller aerial and performance is dependent on a good gain value within the amplifier unit. These aerials are also designed for the reception of UHF signals as well as AM/FM radio transmissions, which eliminates the need for additional aerials.

INDEX